The Golden Door:

The Irony of Our Immigration Policy

THE GOLDEN DOOR:

The Irony of
Our Immigration Policy

BY J. CAMPBELL BRUCE

Random House
New York

Acknowledgments

FOR THEIR invaluable help, I am greatly indebted to Stanley V. Anderson, law graduate, University of California; Reinhard Bendix, associate professor of sociology, University of California; Eugene B. Block, former assistant managing editor, San Francisco *Call-Bulletin*; Eugene E. Buffington, Berkeley, California; Ted Finman, president, *Stanford Law Review*; A. M. Hudson and Wesley J. Van Sciver, research physicists, Stanford University; Roderic A. Ireland, San Francisco, California; Stefan A. Riesenfeld, professor of law, University of California; Kevin Wallace, San Francisco *Chronicle*. I am also deeply grateful to the editors of the *Bulletin of the Atomic Scientists* for kind permission to use material from their special issue of October, 1952, devoted to American visa policy.

To my parents

ALEXANDER AND NORA McCUTCHEON BRUCE

who were immigrants

Not like the brazen giant of Greek fame,
With conquering limbs astride from land to land,
Here at our sea washed, sunset gates shall stand
A mighty woman with a torch, whose flame
Is the imprisoned lightning and her name,
Mother of Exile. From her beacon hand
Glows world wide welcome;
Her mild eyes command the air bridged harbor that twin cities
    frame.

"Keep ancient land your storied pomp!" she cries,
With silent lips. "Give me your tired, your poor,
"Your huddled masses, yearning to breathe free,
"The wretched refuse of your teeming shore.
"Send these, the homeless, the tempest-tossed to me;
"I lift my lamp beside the golden door."

—Lines by Emma Lazarus on the Statue of Liberty.

Purpose

The purpose of this book can be stated briefly—a strike at injustice. I have no sympathy for despotism in any form. I abhor the tyranny of Communism. I also abhor the tyranny that is implicit in our present immigration law and explicit in its administration.

Several persons have asked me, "Do you want to open the gates wide to every Tom, Dick and Harry?" My answer is, No.

There must be an overall annual limit to immigration. There must be a screening process to keep out undesirables, especially Communist agents. But that should not rule out a fair and just treatment of the *bona-fide* immigrant and the visitor to our shores.

Let us offer such people hospitality, not hostility. To do that we need an immigration law that is not written in fear, nor rooted in racial discrimination. And those who administer the law need a change of attitude toward the immigrant and the visitor, an attitude that is not cynical, malevolent and beyond all regard for due process.

I have tried to show why the present immigration law is a bad law by citing examples of what is being done under it in this land of the free. These examples, shocking as they may seem, are not rare; they blot the official record, multiplied a thousandfold. Because of justifiable fears on their part, I was forced to rechristen some of the people in this book. Only by such reassurance were they willing to talk.

J. CAMPBELL BRUCE

Chapter

1   To look at George Wittsack, you'd never take him for the ulcerous type. He is young, only twenty-four; small and compactly built, he has the open countenance of a choir boy. He doesn't smoke, and he doesn't drink, and he has a fine job.

Yet George tosses in his sleep—once he gets to sleep—and a good meal brings on nervous indigestion. In the past few months he has lost ten pounds.

Worry does it. George is being deported—to a country he has never seen.

His mother, stepfather and half-sister live in America.

George was born in Shanghai, of a German father and a White Russian mother. That makes him a native of China, but a German national.

His mother, Lidia, a vivacious blonde, was born in Harbin, where her parents fled at the outbreak of the Bolshevist Revolution. Her father, a Cossack officer of the Czarist Guard, fought the Bolshevists in a bitter withdrawal to Siberia, then escaped with his family into Manchuria. He slipped back into Siberia to rescue three sons still in the fight, and vanished completely. The sons, captured in a last-ditch battle at the Czarist Academy in Sverdlosk, were executed.

Lidia was touring China with a ballet troupe in 1926 when she met and married Frederick Wittsack, a wealthy Shanghai importer-exporter. Three years after George was born they were divorced. To support the child, Lidia sang in night clubs.

Ten years later Lidia married Captain Francisco Montanaro, an Italian skipper. He refused to work for the Japanese when they took Shanghai during World War II, and was hustled off to a concentration camp near Mukden.

After the war George visited his Aunt Sandra in Tsingtao, then an American naval base. She was married to Lieutenant Earl Vroman of the United States Navy, a veteran of both the Normandy and Okinawa invasions. She persuaded George to stay and attend the American high school in Tsingtao.

At the urging of a teacher, who was a graduate of the University of Arizona, George wrote to the university and received a certificate to enroll for the fall term of 1947. He went at once to the American consul to inquire about a student visa. The consul curtly told him he didn't stand a chance for any kind of a visa to the United States. Why? He had no passport; the Bonn government of Western Germany was not yet in existence.

"If I allow you, a stateless person, to go to the United States as a student, what will happen at the end of the four years?" the consul asked. "Where would we send you?"

So George, finishing high school, went back to Shanghai

and took a job with the U.S. Army Air Corps, in charge of a special services section under a Lieutenant Bellocio, a fighter pilot.

The political situation was rapidly growing worse, and George's mother begged him to leave China. He eventually obtained a visa to Argentina. And when his Air Corps job folded in December of 1948—the Communists were approaching Shanghai, and the Army was abandoning its installations and evacuating personnel—George applied to the American consul for a transit visa. He wanted to stop off in San Francisco, en route to South America, to visit his Aunt Sandra, who had been able to come to the United States as the wife of a naval officer.

It took George two months to get his transit visa, allowing him twenty-eight days in the United States. He left Shanghai in February, 1949, aboard the *Luxemburg Victory* and arrived at San Francisco on March 26.

"I can remember the hour—three o'clock in the afternoon," he recalls. "It was a clear day, a beautiful day, and the Golden Gate Bridge looked so strong, so gigantic. A girl stood on the bridge looking down and waving. She was wearing red pedal pushers—I'll never forget that; it was like a picture I'd seen in a magazine.

"The trees on the hills of the Presidio, they looked so funny. They were short, and they all leaned away from the sea. And all the white houses, climbing the hills in neat rows. Color everywhere. I was enchanted. And when I came ashore and saw the streets—they were so clean! All this cleanliness, and beauty, I couldn't believe it. I thought, *what a wonderful place to live!"*

An immigration inspector checked his visa, to which was attached a travel document in lieu of a passport, listing him as "stateless, of German origin." The inspector found all in order and cleared him.

There was a joyous reunion on the dock with his aunt and uncle. And on the way home, Aunt Sandra said, "George, I want you to stay here and go to school."

"I can't," George said. "It's against immigration rules."

"It won't hurt to ask about it," she said.

The next day they went down to the district immigration headquarters and there talked to an Inspector Cole who, George says, was courteous and helpful. Inspector Cole asked if he had ever applied for admission to an American university, and George produced the old certificate from the University of Arizona.

"See if they will accept you again," said the inspector. "If they will, you go on to school. We'll change your status to that of a student."

George wrote to Tucson and was immediately accepted, even though it was the middle of the term. He enrolled, applied himself assiduously, and soon caught up with his classmates. He was making straight "A" grades when, near the end of May—only a few weeks until the close of the term—he was notified to report at once to the immigration office in San Francisco.

Returning to San Francisco, he was told his application for a change of status had been denied. He thereupon requested admission to the United States as a Displaced

Person. He could qualify because he was listed as a stateless person and had entered the country five days before the DP Act expired. He was permitted to apply for such status.

Inspector Cole placed him under technical arrest. George registered for Selective Service, as required by law, then took a job with an insurance firm.

Near the end of 1949 George learned that his mother, stepfather and little half-sister Anita, who had been trapped in Shanghai by the Communists, had managed to bribe their way out to Hong Kong. There they were awaiting immigrant visas to come to the United States, under the Italian quota.

In October of 1950, while he was still anxiously waiting action on his application for DP status, George was ordered to report for a physical. He passed it, was then ordered to report for induction on December 15th. He informed the draft board of his doubtful status as an alien, and a clerk called Immigration to inquire about George's case. The clerk relayed the reply: "It's O.K. for him to be drafted."

At Fort Ord, where he took his basic training, George reported his alien status to the Counter Intelligence Corps. CIC checked with the immigration office at San Francisco and got the word: "Keep him in the Army."

"I didn't want to be there under false pretenses," George says. "But from then on I was solid—a member of the U. S. Armed Forces."

George spoke four languages fluently—English, German, Russian, Chinese. And so, after basic training, he was sent to the military intelligence school at Fort Meade, Maryland. On off-duty hours he worked as a waiter to earn extra money to send to his mother in Hong Kong. The Reds had taken all their possessions. "All our lives," George says, "we have lost everything to the Commies."

His application for DP status was still pending, and that began to worry him. One day Private Wittsack took a bus to Washington and presented his case to Senator Richard Nixon of California, now Vice President. Senator Nixon got in touch with Immigration, and George's file was transferred from San Francisco to Baltimore. But nothing happened.

When he finished intelligence school, George volunteered for Korean duty and was immediately ordered overseas. That was in November, 1951. Before embarking at Seattle, he went again to Immigration and laid the matter before a high district official, a former Army colonel.

"I asked him," George says, "if by fighting in Korea, would I ever be deported? I told him frankly that it seemed silly to go overseas and fight for America if I was to be deported.

"He laughed. Then he got angry at me for asking such a silly question. He said, 'You go right ahead and fight, sonny. And don't worry about deportation. I assure you that will never happen. We are human here—not sadists. We don't operate that way."

It was a dreary, gray day when the troop ship pulled out of Seattle, to the farewell strains of a military band. To a kid of twenty-three, who had no native land he could then call his own, it all had an ominous feeling.

He recalls that day with an understandable touch of bit-
terness: "If I came back dead, I would come back under an
American flag—good enough to be buried in American
soil. But it turned out I came back alive—and not good
enough to live on it."

While George was on the high seas headed for Korea,
his family was on the high seas headed for San Francisco.
After a two-year wait in Hong Kong, his mother, stepfather and half-sister had obtained visas. They were admitted to permanent residence in the United States and
look forward to becoming citizens.

After only several days in Japan, George was sent to
Korea as a replacement in the intelligence section of the
45th Division at Eighth Army headquarters, where he was
entrusted with top-secret material. He occasionally went
up to observation posts—in front of the front lines—on
both Heartbreak Ridge and Baldy.

"Don't get me wrong," he cautions. "I'm no hero. And
I don't want to pretend I am. I never had any hand-to-
hand fighting. But I did take a risk, because if I'd been
captured and the Chinese Communists found I was not an
American citizen—with Russian blood in me—I would
have been shot as a spy. Still, it was only a risk."

He spent nine months in Korea, then was rotated back
to the States. The two years for which he was drafted were
up. An alien, incidentally, cannot enlist, nor become an
officer, but can be drafted.

"We arrived in San Francisco the day before Thanks-
giving, 1952. A girl sang on the dock, welcoming us home.
I cried like a kid—no fooling, I really cried. But I wasn't

the only one—all the 4000 others on the *General Pope*
cried that day."

His mother was there to greet him—the first he had seen
her in three years. "You can imagine what a happy home-
coming that was!"

He returned a Private First Class, with the Korean Service Medal, the Bronze Service Star, and the United Nations
Service Medal. He was discharged on December 4, 1952.
Actually, it was a transfer to the Reserve, in which he must
serve five years. He now belongs, as a PFC, to the 91st
Infantry Division, Presidio of San Francisco, and must
always carry his 1-C Reserve Selective Service card. "I've
still got an obligation to fulfill in this country," he says.

George reported at once to the immigration office, to
tell them he was back and to ask for permanent residence
status, so that he could apply for naturalization. He
couldn't naturalize as a Korean veteran, because at that
time only alien veterans of World Wars I and II, and those
who had served three years in the peacetime Army, could
become citizens as a reward for service.

After reporting to Immigration, he took a six-day rest,
then went to work for the Bank of America. "I'm not a
liability to this country," he says. "I earn my own bread
and butter. I've got a good job, and I'm a good citizen." As
in everything, he applied himself diligently and soon was
promoted to a supervisor's spot, with fifteen men under
him.

Two and a half months later, Immigration summoned
him. The records had disclosed that his application for DP
status, made nearly three years earlier, and long before he

was sent to Korea, had never been acted upon—and he was still under technical arrest. A hearing officer questioned him for three hours. The verdict:

George was a German citizen, and not stateless. (The Bonn government, in the meantime, had come into existence.) His application for DP status was therefore denied.

That wasn't all. The hearing officer held that George's *intent,* when he obtained the transit visa to pass through the United States en route to Argentina, was to stay here as a student. Therefore, he was unlawfully in the country and subject to deportation.

George was flabbergasted. He retained an attorney, Z. B. Jackson, an immigration lawyer of San Francisco, who appealed to Washington. It came back rubber-stamped: Appeal denied. Even the clerk who stamped it apparently was in a hurry, for the imprint was askew and a bit smeary.

"I was so mad," says George, "I bawled."

Meanwhile, a bill was introduced in Congress to make Korean veterans eligible for citizenship. At Jackson's insistence, a Congressman asked Commissioner of Immigration Argyle R. Mackey to hold off a while on cases such as George's.

Mackey replied to the Congressman: "This service cannot undertake to stay the deportation of a deportable alien in anticipation of action on this bill, notwithstanding the fact that he may have honorably served in the Armed Forces of the United States."

A hearing was held June 17, 1953, to decide where to send George. They couldn't return him to China, the land of his birth, because the United States does not recognize

Communist China. The only place to deport him was Germany, the land of his nationality. And George has never set foot in Germany.

Despite all the factors in his favor—his Korean war service, his family here as permanent residents, his good moral character—Immigration was unbending. No leniency, no mercy. Instead, they placed a new, stiffer "charge" against him—that his *intent* when he came to the United States on a transit visa was to remain, not only as a student, but *permanently*.

Dismayed, Lawyer Jackson obtained a continuance of the case in view of the added charge. Then he asked Congressman John F. Shelley of San Francisco to lend a hand. Shelley introduced a private bill to grant George Wittsack permanent residence. This has the effect of staying his deportation until Congress takes action on the Shelley bill. However, it may take Congress years to get around to George because there are an estimated 1500 such bills in the House. Even then, Congress may turn him down. Either way, he faces an uncertain future, for if Congress grants permanent residence there is still a section in the McCarran Act that bars naturalization if there is a warrant of arrest or deportation outstanding. And George is still under technical arrest, with a deportation charge against him.

Congress did eventually pass a law to permit Korean veterans to naturalize, but George could draw little hope from that. The law applies only to those alien veterans who were in the United States on a permanent residence status before induction or, if here temporarily, had entered lawfully. Immigration authorities hold that George entered unlawfully because he had an intent to stay.

That is why George's nerves have been acting up lately. That is why he can't get a good night's sleep, and has trouble with his digestion. "I exercise to keep in condition," he says resolutely, "because I'm not going to let them break me."

In his case the immigration authorities obviously confused *desire* with *intent*. There is a difference. For instance, a window shopper outside Tiffany's may have a *desire* for the jewels displayed, but an *intent* to refrain from breaking the window and taking them, and the law recognizes the distinction.

George puts it this way: "My desire, when I saw this wonderful country, was to stay and go to school. Who wouldn't have such a desire? But the American consul had told me that was impossible. So my intent, when I got the transit visa, was simply to visit my aunt and go on to Argentina."

George had run the double obstacle course most aliens encounter when they seek either to come to the United States or simply to pass through. These obstacle courses, and they are arduous ones, are the consular service abroad and the Immigration Service at our gates. Both wield an absolute, despotic power—certainly puzzling in the world's leading democracy.

This is the crux of the whole problem: These authorities operate outside due process of law because they deal with persons not fully protected by the Constitution or without access, ordinarily, to publicity media that would lend the weight of public opinion to their cause.

The only reason George Wittsack was able to get even a nibble at American higher learning—and indeed to serve in Korea with our Armed Forces—was the fact that he arrived on a transit visa *before* the McCarran Act went into effect. Among other things, Public Law 414—otherwise known as the McCarran-Walter Act—is much stricter about aliens crossing the United States "in immediate and continuous transit."

Consider a small but enlightening instance: the plight of Mrs. E. V. Blaine, ailing wife of a New Zealand doctor, and their twenty-two-year-old son, Robert. The Blaines went out to New Zealand four years ago. In the summer of 1952, Mrs. Blaine returned to her old home in the south of England for an intended year's visit, which was cut short by illness. Robert, a medical student in England, decided to accompany her on the long journey back to New Zealand.

In view of Mrs. Blaine's illness, they sought the easiest route home—by air, across the United States. They obtained a transit visa. Their flight was carefully planned to avoid any possible delay en route, but an unforeseen interruption happened. Their plane was grounded in Denver for three hours by mechanical trouble. They arrived at San Francisco at 1 A.M. on January 13, 1953—just one hour and one minute after the departure of the Pan American World Airways flight to New Zealand, at 11:59 P.M.

An immigration investigator took the Blaines in tow

at the airport. After some debate, he permitted them to register at a San Francisco hotel.

About ten o'clock that morning immigration authorities routed out the Blaines and hauled them off to detention quarters in a downtown skyscraper. There they were locked up—"like common thieves," Mrs. Blaine later complained to the New Zealand press.

Henry Hankey, the British consul at San Francisco, says Robert Blaine "managed to get in touch with our office, and we rushed down at once." He describes the difficulties encountered: "We spent a long time arguing with the immigration people. Their attitude was one of considerable embarrassment, for it was absurd that ordinary travelers should be treated in this way. But I must say they were acting within the limits of their instructions, and they were quite reasonable and decent about it.

"They telephoned Washington in an effort to get permission for the release of the Blaines but were told no, nothing doing. Next day we called our Embassy in Washington, and they intervened. On account of Mrs. Blaine's medical condition, the local people were authorized to release her, but under guard."

The Blaines had spent a day and night in detention. They were taken to a hotel on January 14th and, until their departure on the next Pan American flight at 11:59 P.M. on January 15th, were under constant surveillance, with guards on eight-hour shifts. They were free to move about the city, accompanied by the guard. Once Robert went into a barber shop to get a haircut; his mother had to go with him and wait, so the guard could keep an eye on both his charges.

But Bruce Barber, district director of immigration at San Francisco, was clearly baffled at the Blaines' reaction to this treatment. "What are they griping about?" he told a reporter. "We gave them our de-luxe suite."

Less baffled, and hotly indignant, were the newspapers of New Zealand and Australia. The American press was equally indignant. The San Francisco *Chronicle* called the detention of the Blaines "simply intolerable to a free people," yet illustrative of "the kind of treatment that the McCarran-Walter law has deliberately arranged for the innocent victims of its sweeping suspicions."

The Blaines were legally in the United States during their air journey from coast to coast. They were acceptable travelers in our midst during the forced three-hour stopover in Denver. Yet, only a few hours later, by virtue of the inconvenient circumstance of missing a plane connection—a circumstance beyond their control—they were suddenly branded as suspicious, dangerous aliens who must be locked up for the security of the nation.

Paul Gillespie, an American citizen, had a tougher go of it. Gillespie, now a photographer of Pond Creek, Oklahoma, was born in Canada in 1903 during a Canadian sojourn of his parents. His father was a native of Lowell, Massachusetts.

Paul was still an infant when the family took up residence in El Paso, Texas. He grew up there, went through El Paso's grammar and high schools, and on to Baylor University. In 1934 he crossed the international bridge at

Detroit to Windsor. When he tried to recross the bridge in 1947, immigration authorities barred him. They demanded proof of citizenship.

There was no record of his father's birth—not at all surprising because the recording of births was not a common practice in the last century. But Gillespie did obtain copies of his father's marriage and death certificates, each setting forth his birthplace as Lowell, Massachusetts.

This failed to satisfy the immigration people. Next, Gillespie obtained copies of his two sisters' American birth records, which listed their father's birthplace as Lowell. As further proof, the sisters furnished affidavits attesting they were indeed his sisters, and he was indeed a child of their father.

Supported by these documents, Gillespie pressed his claim of citizenship before a Board of Special Inquiry at Detroit in 1949. After weeks of haggling, the board rejected Gillespie's plea for entry on the ground he still lacked "sufficient documentary evidence of United States citizenship."

Gillespie, in a sense a man locked out of his own home, did what most spunky Americans would do in such a circumstance. He entered illegally—or can an American, who has never forsaken his birthright, enter his native land illegally?

He visited a sister in New Jersey, then settled in Oklahoma. Two years later Immigration found him. And there ensued a series of incidents appalling in their disregard of the Constitution.

On April 17, 1951, an immigration officer from Kansas

City entered Gillespie's home and arrested him by force of arms—without a warrant of any kind. After depositing Gillespie in the local jail, the inspector telephoned his headquarters for authority to make the arrest. (He was compelled to admit this fact on the witness stand later at Gillespie's hearing.)

The next day Gillespie was transferred to the county jail at Enid for an overnight stay, then taken to Kansas City. And there, in the Jackson County jail, he was served with a warrant of arrest.

A bonding firm was willing to go bail, but the immigration authorities let it be known they did not want Gillespie at liberty. The bonding company shied off. After four months behind bars, without a hearing, Gillespie wrote to the Senators from Oklahoma—and his mail was immediately stopped. Another month passed before Gillespie finally obtained legal counsel, who exerted pressure and got a hearing. It lasted a week, and the hearing officer announced his decision: That Gillespie was a citizen of the United States, that all proceedings should end therewith, and Gillespie be freed.

He was released on "conditional parole" and ordered to report monthly to the immigration office at Kansas City, while the case was reviewed by the Commissioner of Immigration in Washington. The Commissioner ordered a further investigation.

That was in October, 1951. Nothing happened until April, 1952. Gillespie was then summoned to the courthouse at Enid for a "reopening of the hearing." (The principle of double jeopardy does not exist in immigration procedures.) This session lasted only forty-five minutes, and the decision was almost identical to that handed down at Kansas City.

Again the case went to Washington for another review by the Commissioner. A month passed. And then the Commissioner advised Gillespie's counsel to certify the case to the Board of Immigration Appeals in Washington for final decision. This entailed a costly preparation of a brief, mailed in May. Three months later the Board notified Gillespie's lawyer that the decision of the hearing officer was affirmed, and the case closed.

Thus, after five troubled years, during which Gillespie says he was "hounded like a thief," he won the right to remain in the country where he rightfully belonged all the time as a citizen, the son of a native.

Due process has long been overdue in the operations of the Immigration Service. Aliens are sometimes held in detention for unusual lengths of time—without a hearing, without even a charge placed against them.

Peter Nicolof, a stateless Bulgarian musician, was head of the string department at the South China Conservatory of Music in Fukien. He fled at the approach of the Communists and spent two years at the International Refugee Organization camp on the island of Samar, the Philippines. He was granted a visa after a thorough screening by the State Department, and his entry was sponsored by the National Catholic Welfare Conference. Yet, when he arrived at San Francisco he was locked up in detention quarters in a downtown federal office building. He was held there fourteen months without a hearing, without even a charge against him. When a writ of habeas corpus was sought in federal court, Immigration abruptly decided his entry would not imperil the nation after all.

Valentina Gardner, pretty White Russian wife of an American combat veteran, came to the United States under the War Brides Act. She was carefully screened by both the State Department and the Counter Intelligence Corps before she left Japan. Nevertheless, immigration authorities seized her at San Francisco and held her prisoner in the federal office building for thirteen months. Her case eventually got into the newspapers and caused a public outcry. On the eve of her second Christmas in America—the first one a dreary holiday season behind barred windows in this land of liberty her husband had so often extolled—she was released on bail by court order, over the bitter opposition of the Immigration Service. Twenty months after her arrival Immigration finally decided this girl posed no threat to the United States.

Several hundred wives of Chinese-American war veterans, arriving under the provisions of the same act, were held incommunicado for many months. Even their husbands were denied visiting privileges. The wife of one veteran committed suicide.

Scores of White Russians, many fleeing Communism a second time—the Bolshevists in Russia, then the Chinese Reds—were held for periods of eight months and more before Immigration determined they were not suspect.

Countless instances of almost incredible cruelty and injustice stain the history of our Immigration Service. Instead of a hospitality house at our ports of entry for *bona*

fide guests and future citizens, we have a prison, euphe-
mistically called detention quarters. The refugee, already
screened and bearing a visa, sails with glorious dreams of
freedom and opportunity—only to glimpse America
through barred windows for months, even years, and he
never knows why. Uncle Sam becomes not the genial host
he was led to believe by the Voice of America, but a ruthless jailer.

The loss of United States prestige abroad, now at its
lowest postwar ebb, may be attributed in part to the shabby
treatment our consular officials accord visa applicants,
many of them distinguished scientists invited to address
American societies.

The fault lies squarely with our immigration laws. They
were bad enough in the past, but the worst features of the
past laws, and many new restrictions, were wrapped up in
Public Law 414, which was enacted on June 27, 1952, and
went into effect on December 24th of the same year. This
is the Immigration and Nationality Act of 1952, or the Mc-
Carran-Walter Act, commonly known as the McCarran
Act.

In September, 1952, President Truman, who had vetoed
the McCarran-Walter bill, appointed the President's Commission on Immigration and Naturalization to inquire
into our immigration laws in the light of current world
affairs. On January 1, 1953, the President's Commission
issued its celebrated report, based on testimony from
more than 600 persons and organizations at thirty sessions
around the country, from Boston to San Francisco. The
Commission recommended that the McCarran Act, a mix-

ture of old and new statutes, be rewritten from beginning to end. The foregoing case histories, picked at random, may give you an idea why.

It all poses certain questions: Why should America, founded and brought to greatness by immigrants, look upon the immigrant with such hostility? Why should America, exerting its utmost to spare the free world from the iron-cleated heel, practice its own brand of despotism? Why should America, decrying the merciless police states of the Kremlin, harbor little police states within the framework of its own government?

Let us take a searching look.

Chapter

2 Who made America?

First came the English colonists to the shores of Virginia,
then the Puritans to New England, the Quakers to Pennsylvania, the English Catholics to Maryland. They laid an
enduring foundation here of the English language and
English law.

Succeeding waves of settlers brought from other lands
new customs, new cultures, new crafts—all sturdy materials
to build the walls, the floors, the roof. Thus, in three busy
centuries, was raised the imposing structure that is the
United States of America. Millions of strong hands laid
the bricks and troweled the mortar in between; millions
of eager minds contributed to a living democracy out of
great diversity.

The Dutch carved New Amsterdam out of this early wilderness—the New York of today, where men of all races
and religions live and work and cast their secret ballots.
Lovers of freedom, the Dutch opened their homes to the
first Jewish immigrants, refugees from Portuguese tyranny
in Brazil. French Catholics colonized the Mississippi

Valley; French Protestant exiles, the Huguenots, sank new roots on the Atlantic Seaboard. Toward the end of the seventeenth century came the German Quakers, at the bid of Quaker William Penn, and they were the forebears of the Pennsylvania Dutch. The Spanish came as conquerors of the Southwest and the brown-robed padres brought the Word.

Most of them came, then and later, in flight from religious persecution, political tyranny, economic slavery. The German Quakers had sought a haven of free worship; in 1848 came a host of Germans in quest of political asylum. To the new land flocked masses of Scotch-Irish, themselves an ancestral mixture of Scot, Irish, Briton, Norwegian, Dane. From the Orient came a contribution: the Chinese coolies, imported to supply cheap labor after the Gold Rush. In the decades that ended the last and began this century came the "new" immigrants—successive multitudes of Italians, Austrians, Hungarians, Slavs, Poles, Russians, Lithuanians, Finns, some Irish and Scandinavians.

These were the people who made America—the immigrant sires of today's native-born.

Each group came bearing gifts—a special skill, an industry, a culture—and these offerings went into the common hamper, for the use and benefit of all. Countless individuals came with little more than the rumpled garments they wore, but they had the priceless assets of hardy spirit, character, and the passion for freedom that had spurred them to rip up roots long set in the native heath and seek a better life in the New World. They *had* to be men of will.

Waves of immigration generated their own waves of prosperity, for they made possible the conquest of the wilderness and an ever expanding economy, evidenced today in an American standard of living unmatched anywhere. Even when they came in great batches, these immigrants did not create economic crises. They replaced many workers already on the job, but there were better jobs available for the replaced workers. For immigration acted like a catalytic agent on the American economy. Each worker-immigrant brought along his family, and that signified more buying. Greater buying power meant greater demand for goods; greater demand for goods meant greater production; greater production meant a greater labor market.

This was recognized in the early days of the Republic. James Madison told the Constitutional Convention in 1787: "That part of America which has encouraged them (the foreigners) has advanced most rapidly in population, agriculture, and the 'arts.' "

That has held true ever since. Department of Commerce statistics show that today the Northeast region of the United States, with the highest percentage of foreign born, 13.1 per cent, has the highest per capita income, $1690. The South Central region, with the lowest percentage of foreign born, 1.5 per cent, has the lowest per capita income, $1030.

In the 145 years of our history from 1776 to 1921, when the first ceiling was placed on immigration, the welcome mat was out generally to all who had the price of the passage. A man was not asked to bring more than a strong back and willing hands. The first federal immigration statute, enacted during Lincoln's administration, fostered immigration.

As time went on there came a need to take a closer look at the immigrants and to sift out the undesirables. And so, in 1882, a law was passed to exclude the pauper, the criminal, and the diseased. That same year saw passage of the Chinese Exclusion Act, extended in 1917 to most Orientals in a so-called Asiatic Barred Zone then set up.

The 1917 Immigration Act codified all the laws that had gone before and added a few restrictions of its own, the most controversial a literacy test for aliens over sixteen years of age. (This is a fact: our most literate are the native-born whites of foreign parentage, not the native-born whites of native-born parents.) The McCarran Act, in its codification, picks up from 1917; wraps all the intervening statutes into one big unwieldy package; tightens up old restrictions, and tacks on a few score more.

The first limit on immigration came in 1921, brought on by various factors. We had experienced a European war, and an isolationist reaction set in. We listened to whispers that Europe was making ready to dump millions of undesirables onto our shores—though how, with so many vessels sent to the bottom of the Atlantic by the German U-boats, was never a part of the whisper. The alarm spread that the United States, populated by 106 million people, was already "filled up." (Back in colonial days, when the population was less than three million, the same alarm was raised, but ignored.) In the brief postwar economic collapse, labor felt a deep concern over job security—immigrants might put Americans out of work. The ugliest factor of all—one that fired widespread antipathy toward immigration—was the rise of Ku Klux Klan with its rampant racial and religious prejudices.

Out of this turbulence came the first quota system. This quota system was a curious contrivance that limited the annual flow of immigrants of any nationality to a percentage of the number of persons of that nationality reported living in the United States in a particular year. The 1921 Act set the group limit at 3 per cent, on the basis of the 1910 census, and fixed the overall ceiling for immigration in any year at 357,803. Thus emerged a type of thinking contrary to American traditions, but dignified by legislative edict—the theory that what counted was not the man, but where he came from.

From then on the golden door began to stick. The Act of 1924 closed it to a point barely ajar, by reducing the limit further from 3 to 2 per cent, and setting the 1890 census, rather than the 1910 census, as a base—a direct slap at the peoples of Eastern and Southern Europe, who had come in greatest numbers after 1890. The ceiling was lowered to 164,667 per year.

Into the 1924 Act mysteriously slipped the national origins formula—an amendment that was sort of an afterthought, eliciting scarcely a thousand words of debate, but since then evoking millions of epithets. This formula, effective five years later, in 1929, adapted the quotas to the *national origins* of the people making up the population of the United States in a given year. The given year was 1920.

Here was the parlor-puzzle way they figured it out: The quota of any nationality during any fiscal year "shall be a number which bears the same ratio to 150,000 as the number of inhabitants in the continental United States in 1920, having that national origin, bears to the number of inhabitants in the continental United States in 1920, but that the minimum quota of any nationality shall be 100." Get it? Then read it again. Now, once more. It will come to you, with patience.

There were several jokers. In devising this weird computation, they did not actually count the *total* number of inhabitants in the continental United States in 1920. They did not include immigrants from the Western Hemisphere and their descendants; aliens not eligible for citizenship and their descendants; the descendants of slave immigrants, and American Indians.

Furthermore, they gave a man an origin by the name he bore. Thus, into the English-origin hopper went many a Smith and Jones who, for understandable reasons, had legally changed their names from the tongue-twisters that characterize so many Slavic names.

Nor did the law really mean a quota for any nationality. It said so, yes, but there still existed the bar to Orientals. Not until 1943 was the Chinese Exclusion Act repealed. Three years later Filipinos and natives of India were granted the privilege of entering. The present McCarran Act removed the bars to all other Orientals and accorded naturalization privileges to all races. (Incidentally, in 1940 all American Indians and Eskimos were finally awarded citizenship in the land where they've lived since time immemorial.)

The minimum quotas fixed in the 1929 amendment boosted the annual immigration limit above the 150,000 ceiling used for computations. The total was now 153,714 a year.

But the lawmakers were not through yet. The framers of the McCarran Act came up with still another set of quotas, based on the national origins formula. However, their mathematicians evolved "a mechanically simplified formula for determining the annual quota for each quota area (the term 'quota area' is substituted for the term 'nationality' as being more appropriate) which provides that the quota for each quota area will be one-sixth of 1 per cent of the number of inhabitants in the continental United States in 1920 attributable by national origin to that quota area." But they borrowed the old tables to determine the number of foreign born in the United States representing each quota area. The annual ceiling was upped a little, to 154,657.

Although the McCarran Act removes racial bars to immigration, it still advocates discrimination by retaining this national-origins system. To people abroad it seems inconsistent that America in one breath should proclaim the brotherhood of man and in the next breath espouse a national policy that denies such a brotherhood.

The discriminatory formula of national origin did not creep into the law by accident; it was put there by design, as we shall see later. Along with it goes the current fear that a subversive might sneak into our midst in the guise of a refugee—yet Soviet agents can enter the country freely on diplomatic missions. This fear has helped to create a hostile attitude toward any and all immigrants.

Actually, there is nothing new in this hostility. At one time or another in our history the children of immigrants have resented new immigrants, particularly of a different race. Often enough an immigrant came, found America to his liking, then wanted the door closed on all others. The fisherman had found a good hole.

Go back over the years. The Ku Klux Klan of the First World War period pre-dated Hitler with a preachment of Nordic superiority and anti-Semitism, plus anti-Catholicism. But the American Protective Association of the 1890's beat the Ku Klux Klan to such rabble-rousing. The Irish and German groups—themselves the target of the Know-Nothing Party's anti-foreign fomentations—snarled at the Slavs and the Italians who came later. The Chinese coolie was imported for cheap labor, then the "Yellow peril!" cry went up, and the Chinese were shut out altogether.

Go further back into our beginnings. In the pre-Revolution days many colonies passed laws against "Papists" and Jews. Lord Baltimore's Maryland colony, founded by Catholic liberals fleeing persecution, welcomed refugees of all faiths; in time rebels took over and excluded Catholic immigrants. Roger Williams fled religious abuse in Massachusetts, itself the haven of Puritans who had fled

England for the same reason. Even the Quakers, after settling Pennsylvania, looked with disdain on certain types of immigrant, but today the Quakers are in the foreranks of the fight against the McCarran Act.

And so this current phenomenon is neither new nor strange. Over the decades it has risen and subsided, like waves that crest and fall away. As Solomon said, This too shall pass. But not of its own accord; it must be stamped out, as were all the others, by action of the people.

We can look with amusement today on Cotton Mather's effort to keep out William Penn, the revered founder of Pennsylvania. This is what the good Reverend, leader of the Massachusetts Bay Colony, wrote in 1682:

"To Ye Aged and Beloved, Mr. John Higginson:
"There be now at sea a ship called Wellcome, which has on board one hundred or more of the heretics and malignants called Quakers, with W. Penn, who is the chief scamp, at the head of them. The General Court has accordingly given secret orders to Master Malachi Huscott, of the brig Porpoise, to waylay the said Wellcome slyly as near the Cape of Cod as may be, and make captive the said Penn and his ungodly crew, so that the Lord may be glorified and not mocked on the soil of this new country with the heathen worship of these people. Much spoil can be made by selling the whole lot to Barbadoes, where slaves fetch good prices in rum and sugar, and we shall not only do the Lord great service by punishing the wicked, but we shall make great good for His Minister and people.
"Yours in the bowels of Christ,
"Cotton Mather."

Yes, it is amusing now. But that very thing was given modern dress in the McCarran Act, which went into effect —with perfect timing for irony—on Christmas Eve, 1952.

The difference between it and the older expressions of bigotry is that the older ones were not voted into law as national policy.

Chapter

3

"TIFLIS . . . The great bulk of emigrants to the U.S. from this district are highly undesirable as material for future American citizens. They are not only illiterate, but the years of unsettled conditions which they have been forced to live have caused them to lose the habit of work. Their physical and moral courage is greatly depleted, as well as their physical constitutions. The bulk of them have been habituated either to lawlessness or to the exercise of violence in the name of the law for so long that if not actually impregnated with Bolshevism they are good material for Bolshevik propaganda.

"Our restrictions on immigration should be so rigid that it would be impossible for most of these people to enter the United States. Reference is especially made to Armenians, Jews, Persians, and Russians of the ordinary classes, all of which have been so driven hither and thither since 1914 that they cannot be regarded as desirable population for any country . . ."

Abstract from a State Department report incorporated in the House committee's report accompanying HR 4075, which became the Immigration Act of 1921.

That was official doctrine. Let's look at one of the men who was in Tiflis, wanting to come to America, when the law was passed. His story is typical of the countless thousands of immigrants, and thousands upon thousands of Displaced Persons, who have made such a smooth adjustment to American life. It accents the needlessness of the current fears of immigration, for it reveals two old ponderables: What America means to the immigrant, and what the immigrant means to America.

George Mardikian, an Armenian, was born in Tiflis, capital of Caucasian Georgia, in 1903. At the age of three he was taken by his family to Constantinople (now Istanbul) where his father, a trader, had a branch office.

In the next decade and a half young George lived through several lifetimes of horror. He was only five when the young Turks came to power with the fall of the Red Sultan, followed by the 1909 massacre of Armenian Christians in Cilicia. "I remember," he says, "the people coming into the churches with their arms cut off, and their ears cut off, and their legs cut off by the Turk scimitars." And then, in quick succession, came the chaotic periods of the Italian-Turkish War in 1911, the Balkan uprising in 1912 that slashed into Turkey, and the First World War. The family fled back to Tiflis in 1915, escaping the greatest massacre in history, the slaughter of a million and a half Armenians in Turkey.

Armenia, called the "Little Ally," became a Republic at the end of the First World War, realizing a dream of nearly seven centuries. But it was a short-lived Republic. In November of 1920 the Bolsheviks took over Armenia with the aid of the Turks. The Armenians, sickened by the atrocities that occurred, ejected the Bolsheviks and re-established the Republic the following February. This second Republic was even shorter-lived. Three months later the Bolsheviks seized little Armenia again, and it remains a Soviet vassal today.

In 1920, while Armenia was a Republic, young George went to Captain Eddie Fox, then district director of Near East Relief at Kars. George wanted to start a Boy Scout movement in Armenia. He recalls that meeting: "Captain Fox pointed to a picture on the wall of a funny-looking man. In our country grown men wore a full flowing beard and a big mustache. Here was a man with a short beard and *no* mustache. Captain Fox pointed to him and said, 'What Armenia needs is a man like him—an Abe Lincoln.'

"I had read about Abe Lincoln, but had never seen a picture of him. I felt suddenly in his presence—such awe and reverence. Even today that feeling comes over me when I go to the Lincoln Memorial in Washington. I reach for my hat as I walk up the steps, and as I go in there, in the presence of this great, great soul, tears fill my eyes. It is the same with other people. Outside they speak loud, but inside, they whisper."

George Mardikian arrived in New York by ship on July 24, 1922, a penniless young man of nineteen. He was taken directly to Ellis Island for processing.

"They gave me a big cake of soap and a great big Turkish towel and told me to take a shower. They had hot and cold water, and nobody was afraid to use too much of it. I thought I had landed in heaven.

"There, in the suds and hot water, was washed away everything that belonged to the other side of the world—

the hatred and animosity, all that was ugly. I felt born again. Under that shower I became already an American, before the five years were up."

Next day he was taken to Grand Central Station to board a train for San Francisco, where an older brother and a married sister lived.

Mardikian did not arrive literally penniless. He came with perhaps more pennies than any other immigrant in history. His brother had sent him a $5 bill and on the boat a passenger had "sold" him $5 worth of pennies. Waiting for him in New York, also from his brother, were the train ticket and $25 for meals. "I brought $20 of it to my brother, because I didn't know how to order food on the train. I ate potato salad for seven days."

Young George's first job in America was washing dishes in Coffee Dan's, an oldtime San Francisco night spot. He worked from seven o'clock at night until seven o'clock in the morning, with every other Sunday off. "All immigrants have the idea you just pick the silver dollars off the street. This is a land of opportunity, yes, but for those who make the opportunity. I thought that was a lot of money, $12 a week. I could do so much with it, and I did. I began sending my mother $20 a month.

"Later I found that Clinton's down the street would pay me $13 a week, only six days a week, so I quit and went there. That was terrific—I could change jobs and no trouble about it! Then I found a chain restaurant paid $18 a week, with every other Sunday off, so I went there. I had to work hard, but that was all right. I loved work. Four years later I became manager of the chain.

"I studied nights—or days, when I worked nights—because I wanted to be an American—to walk, talk, think like Americans. My greatest ambition was to be a genuine American, so the people who were so nice to me would be proud of me. The greatest insult was to call me a foreigner. Once a fellow worker called me that, and I invited him down in the cellar. He was bigger, but I was mad. I knocked him against a big mirror and smashed it, and I thought, there goes my job. But when the owner found what the trouble was he said, 'Did George give him a good beating?' And the man I beat up said, 'He sure did!' And the owner said, 'Forget about the mirror, George.' And this is also the American way—the fellow I beat up for calling me a foreigner became my best friend."

Eventually George went to Fresno and there opened a small restaurant called Omar Khayyam's, featuring Armenian dishes. It prospered. He kept his eye on the restaurant on O'Farrell Street near Powell in San Francisco where he had washed dishes at $12 a week, and it was a proud day when he bought that place too and established a San Francisco Omar Khayyam's. One of America's most famed chefs, George Mardikian today owns city real estate, two big ranches, a radio station in San Jose devoted largely to public service.

That is what America can mean to an immigrant.

And what can an immigrant mean to America?

"I could have lived comfortably working for my boss," Mardikian says. "But I wanted to contribute something to this wonderful country. I suppose being an immigrant I was given that complex—that I was not equal to others

—so I would be crushed if I could not contribute something. I went on a tour around the world, working and sweating in the most remote kitchens to find rare recipes for America. I even went poking around in the San Lazaro Archives, in Venice, and found an ancient book, the story of Armenian cuisine. I took foods of the East and changed them to the palates of America."

The great and the humble have beaten a path to the exotic restaurant of this immigrant, now a proud American citizen. During World War II no wounded soldier, sailor or marine could pay for a meal in Omar Khayyam's, and even today a war wounded eats on the house.

After the war, at the request of the War Department, Mardikian went to Europe to survey the food and food-supply situation of the occupation forces in France, Germany, Italy and the low countries. General Omar Bradley told him: "George, the biggest medal you got from the Army is that everything you suggested we put into effect."

He eliminated waste and abolished the hated KP duty in the Army. "By punishing one man, they punished the whole company. He didn't like what he was doing, so he did all he could to get even. I tried to inject into the Armed Forces, from generals down to privates, the idea that cooking is an honorable profession. A man must have a love of doing it. Now men who *ask* for it get that duty, and they do a wonderful job because there is the reward of promotion."

He put years of professional restaurant experience into his survey, which was later duplicated in Korea. And so today the GI eats better, and the government saves millions of dollars a year—because of a penniless Armenian immigrant from Tiflis named George Mardikian.

And it didn't cost the American taxpayers one dime. It was all on George.

On his desk is a framed photograph inscribed: "To George Mardikian—with appreciation of valuable services to the U.S. Army and with best wishes. Dwight D. Eisenhower."

On his first European tour for the Army (he made his third tour in 1952), Mardikian discovered thousands of his former countrymen in DP camps. He told them: "I will see to it that our people in America are completely informed of your plight. I promise."

He kept that promise. With S. M. Saroyan, a San Francisco lawyer, he organized the American National Committee to Aid Homeless Armenians (ANCHA). They made many speaking tours through the United States and Canada at their own expense, enlisting support. And when the 1948 Displaced Persons program was authorized by Congress, ANCHA was ready to sponsor 3,000 Armenian DP's.

"Some settled in California," Mardikian relates, "and one day I asked them what was the most impressive thing in America. The skyscrapers of our cities, the great mountains, the vastness of America? No. On their bus trip from New York to California, they made over 200 stops—and not a single policeman came up and said, 'Let me see your passport.'"

Tiflis, a beautiful city with an Artists Theater that was once the cultural hub of the Caucasus, made other contributions to America. Danielian, the ballet dancer, came from Tiflis, and so did Tamara Toumanova, the ballerina and actress. Ruben Mamoulian, the famed director of film and stage successes, was born in Tiflis. So was Akim Tamiroff, the actor.

In 1941 George Mardikian was invited to New York to appear on the "We the People" radio program. Newspaper reporters showed up at his hotel.

"Before we have a press conference," Mardikian told them, "I want to visit my favorite shrine and say a prayer. They were all astonished—my favorite shrine right there in New York? They were curious, so they all came along.

"We went over to Bedloe Island. I tell you, they had lumps in their throat. There were six reporters, and only two had ever been there. Right at the base, where those wonderful lines are written, I said:

"'Gentlemen, you have no conception what this means to a man like me, who came here from tyranny and everything that is bad. This is a shrine that should live forever.'"

The shrine, of course, is the Statue of Liberty.

Chapter

4   Sponsors of the McCarran Act proclaim it as a mere codification of all the immigration statutes enacted over the years. True, it repealed forty-eight previous laws and amended ten others. But it did more than that. It retained too many old injustices and added more than a hundred new restrictive features.

Here, indeed, was a long-overdue opportunity to codify and clarify all that had gone before, to streamline and shape the welter of statutes to the changing times, to root out all the racial evils that sully American tradition, and, most importantly, to make our immigration policies conform with United States leadership and goals in the world of today.

Congress had plenty of time—five years—to do a real job. It expended enough energy to enact a law that would trumpet abroad, in forthright language even Russia could not distort: "We mean what we say, when we say we believe in the brotherhood of man."

But Congress muffed its chance. The mountain labored and brought forth malice. Into this 302-page omnibus bill Congress packed all the hypocrisy, the malevolence, the arrogance, the racial resentments of earlier laws and earlier moods. It scoffed at the self-evident truth set forth in the Declaration of Independence—that all men are created equal.

Congress flouted this sacred credo by keeping alive as a national policy the long-damned Ku Klux Klan theory of white supremacy, espoused in the quota system that makes a man's national origin count, not the man himself. Most Americans prefer to forget the violent rashes that blemish our history—the Native American Party of 1835, the Know-Nothings of 1850, the American Protective Association of 1890, the anti-Catholic, anti-Semitic, anti-Negro Ku Klux Klan of most recent memory. They are no longer skeletons locked away in a back closet; they've been dragged forth into the daylight, to rattle their bones in Public Law 414.

The national origins quota formula rings hollow as a counterfeit coin beside the solid substance of George Washington's utterance in 1783: "The bosom of America is open to receive not only the opulent and respectable stranger but the oppressed and persecuted of all nations and religions; whom we shall welcome to a participation of all our rights and privileges, if by decency and propriety of conduct they appear to merit the enjoyment."

The National Council of Churches of Christ says the formula is "an affront to the conscience of the American people." The Archbishop of the Catholic Archdiocese of Boston says it "cannot be defended without recourse to the discredited and un-Christian tenets of racism." The Synagogue Council of America says it "flies arrogantly in the face of everything we know and have learned, and stands as a gratuitous affront to the peoples of many regions of the world." They were joined in testimony before the President's Commission by spokesmen from the arts, the sciences, the professions, education, agriculture, business, law, labor, and social service, by civic leaders and individuals.

Despite such a preponderance of testimony, Senator Pat McCarran, Democrat of Nevada, insists the law he coauthored "does not contain one iota of racial or religious discrimination."

The Senate group considering retention of the formula reported: "Without giving credence to any theory of Nordic superiority, the subcommittee believes that the adoption of the national origins formula was a rational and logical method of numerically restricting immigration in such a manner as to best preserve the sociological and cultural balance in the population of the United States."

Let us go back and look at the record of that adoption.

Senator David A. Reed, Republican, the gentleman from Pennsylvania who tacked the formula onto the 1924 Act, bluntly expressed to his colleages the intent behind it: "I think most of us are reconciled to the idea of discrimination. I think the American people want us to discriminate; and I don't think discrimination in itself is unfair . . . We have got to discriminate."

The House majority report on that 1924 bill stated: "If immigration from southern and eastern Europe may enter the United States on a basis of substantial equality with that admitted from the older sources of supply . . . the racial preponderance must in time pass to those elements of the population who reproduce more rapidly on a lower standard of living than those possessing other ideals."

Congressman Addison T. Smith, Republican of Idaho, warned: "If there is not a stringent restriction on Greek immigration to the United States, it is predicted by well-known authorities that in five years the Greeks will have complete monopoly of our lines of profitable business with which people of other nationalities cannot successfully compete."

It may come as a surprise to learn that the State Department in 1924 supported these racist views. Here are excerpts from only a few of the State Department warnings attached to the House majority report on the 1924 bill:

"WARSAW   Attention is directed to the character of the majority of the persons who are now leaving Poland for the United States . . . It is only too obvious that they must be subnormal, and their normal state is of very low standard . . ."

"BUCHAREST   A large number of undesirable aliens are applying for permission to proceed to the United States . . . being as a class economic parasites, tailors, small salesmen, butchers, etc. . . . The severest kind of control should be exercised over these immigrants from central Europe as this type of immigrant is not desirable from any point of view at this time."

"ITALY   A large proportion of aliens from this district going to the United States are inimical to the best interests of the American Government. This is not due to any Bolshevist or Communist tendency on their part, but to their standards of living and their characteristics, which render them unassimilable. Practically all the immigrants from this district are of the peasant class. For the most part they are small in stature and of a low order of intelligence."

"ROTTERDAM   The great mass of aliens passing through Rotterdam at the present time are Russian Poles or Polish Jews of the usual ghetto type. Most of them are frankly getting out of Poland to avoid war conditions. They are filthy, un-American, and often dangerous in their habits."

Congressman Emanuel Celler, Democrat of New York, who was a member of Congress in 1924 at the time the national origins formula was adopted, told the President's Commission: "It [the formula] was deliberately adopted to proscribe not only southern and eastern Europeans, but also Catholics and Jews. That is the unvarnished truth. I heard it stated time and time again on the floor of the House, and I have been battling ever since to wipe out that abomination. I called it that before and I call it that now with greater emphasis.

"As you know, this national origin theory is practically parallel to Hitler's theory of racial superiority: the Herrenvolk versus the Slav race. We say to the peoples of northern and western Europe, 'You are the master race: you are the Herrenvolk race; we want you to come in; we beckon you; we give you every opportunity to come in.' In the other breath we say to the people of central, eastern, and southern Europe, 'You are the Slavic race; we don't want you; you are riffraffs.' That is contrary to all we hold sacred and dear in this country.

"You take the list of casualties that comes out of Korea . . . You find all manner and kind of names. You find names of boys who came, or whose fathers and mothers or forebears came from southern and eastern Europe. The bombs and bullets know no racial discrimination."

Margaret Mead, one of America's best-known anthropologists, told the President's Commission: "All human beings from all groups of people have the same potentialities. They may have been barefoot for a hundred thousand years, but there again their capacity to wear shoes is exactly like the people who have been wearing shoes for a hundred thousand years . . . When you add to that that it is on the whole the enterprising who emigrate and those who care more about freedom and are willing to risk their skins for freedom in many parts of eastern Europe, you realize that any such point of view is artificial and cuts off good ancestors for our great-great-grandchildren. We want that ancestor in good human stocks from wherever it comes in the world."

The great irony is that we expended billions of dollars and countless thousands of young lives not so long ago to wipe out the very thing now fostered in this act—the Hitlerian theory of Nordic superiority.

Representative Francis E. Walter, Democrat of Pennsylvania, who shares the title of the 1952 Act with Senator McCarran, boasts nevertheless that this is "the most liberal immigration law in U. S. history." And he shores up his boast: "For the first time, all racial bars to immigration are removed. Asiatic countries are given immigration quotas determined by the same formula as quotas for Europe. For the first time, all racial bars to naturalization are removed."

Anyone less intent on selling Mr. Walter's product might ask: Should we brag that we waited until the year 1952 to let down racial barriers to immigration and naturalization? They might ask: Would it not better fit our greatness if instead we offered humble apologies to these people we so long and so grievously affronted? President Franklin D. Roosevelt did so when he characterized the Chinese Exclusion Act, upon its repeal in 1943, as "an historical mistake."

Mr. Walter states flatly that Asiatic countries are given quotas based on the same formula as quotas for Europe. To set him straight on that notion, we refer him to Section 201 (a) of the Act he co-sponsored. It sets forth: "The annual quota of any quota area shall be one-sixth of 1 percentum of the number of inhabitants in the continental United States in 1920, which number, *except for the purpose of computing quotas for quota areas within the Asia-Pacific triangle*, shall be the same number heretofore determined under the provisions of section 11 of the Immigration Act of 1924, attributable by national origin to such quota area." (Italics mine.)

We have seen how frankly outspoken is the discrimination against Southern and Eastern Europe. We shall now see how much deeper is the discrimination against the Asiatic, and particularly against the Chinese.

Public Law 414 sets up its own modified Oriental Exclusion Act by establishing a so-called Asia-Pacific triangle. This triangle embraces twenty-one countries or quota areas ranging from Afghanistan to Japan. Instead of a quota based on the formula used elsewhere, each area in the triangle is given a flat quota of 100, with the exception of Japan (185) and Chinese (105). The quota is supposed to be a flat 100, but it doesn't actually work out that way. If the minimums held true, the total immigration from the triangle would run to 2,190. However, a ceiling of 2,000 is placed on the entire Asia-Pacific triangle, thus reducing the minimums to sub-minimums.

There is an even greater deviation from the formula in the Asia-Pacific triangle. Only for the immigrant of Oriental blood do antecedents play such an unusual role as we find here. An immigrant born *outside* the triangle, whose ancestry is as much as one-half Oriental, is chargeable to an Asiatic quota. For example, if you were born in England of a British father and a Siamese mother, you would come under the Siamese quota. If you were born in Canada of French parents, you would be nonquota as a Canadian citizen; but if one of your parents happened to be Cambodian, you would be a quota Indo-Chinese.

To complicate matters, there is a China quota (100) as well as a Chinese quota (105). A Chinese immigrant is chargeable to the *Chinese* quota wherever he is born—in

China, Denmark, Guatemala or Timbuctoo, and even if half his ancestry be British, Swiss, or any other nationality. But a non-Chinese immigrant born in China comes under the *China* quota. Compounding the discrimination against the Chinese is a situation such as this: a Japanese born in Korea is chargeable to the Korean quota, but a Chinese born in Korea is chargeable to the *Chinese* quota.

Public Law 414 keeps a vigilant eye the world over on 100 per cent Asiatics—parents from different Asian quota countries—who would emigrate to the United States. It sets up a separate Asia-Pacific triangle quota of 100 for this category—persons of mixed Oriental parentage born outside that vast region. For example, an immigrant born in Portugal of a Filipino father and a Burmese mother is chargeable to the separate triangle quota.

In all, this section of the act lists six different classifications to pigeonhole Asiatics.

Former Senator William Benton, Democrat of Connecticut, contrasted this policy with the billions we spend to keep free peoples elsewhere in the fold of freedom: "We can totally destroy that investment, and can ruthlessly and stupidly destroy faith and respect in our great principles, by enacting laws that, in effect, say to the peoples of the world: 'We love you, but we love you from afar. We want you, but, for God's sake, stay where you are.' "

Dean Acheson, former Secretary of State, told the President's Commission that Asia was deeply gratified by the lifting of the bar of exclusion but that "the racial discrimination apparent in the triangle provision can be expected to keep alive some feelings of resentment . . . The combination of very small quotas for Asia and the Asia-Pacific triangle provision still furnish ground for Asian suspicion of United States motives."

Let us scrutinize more closely the quota bias elsewhere. More than two-thirds of *all* quotas, totaling nearly 109,000 of the annual ceiling of 155,000 for *all* quota immigration, go to three countries—Great Britain (65,364), Germany (25,814), and Ireland (17,756).

Next five largest quota countries are Poland (6,488), Italy (5,645), Sweden (3,295), Netherlands (3,136), and France (3,059).

The big quotas go to the countries that don't want them. The smallest quotas go the countries that desperately need them. But the unused quotas of the big-quota countries cannot be transferred to the small-quota countries. They are simply wasted.

In the nineteen years prior to 1948, Great Britain utilized only 151,000 of its allotted 1,248,000 quota numbers; Ireland only 43,000 of its allotted 339,207. This has cut the annual quota immigration to less than half of the 155,000 allowed. Yet the President's Commission heard expert testimony to the effect that the United States could easily absorb 250,000 immigrants a year. Actually, during the decade of the 'thirties, more people left the United States than came in.

As a result of the wastage in quota numbers, some countries have waiting lists that extend into the next several centuries. For instance, Greece, with a quota of 310 per year, has a backlog of more than 24,000. A Greek who applies today for a quota visa will have a wait of eighty years.

Although Great Britain uses such a small percentage of her large assignment of quota numbers, the McCarran Act sets up subquotas of 100 for each of the British colonies in the Western Hemisphere. This ostensibly applies to whites and Negroes alike, but its practical effect is the partial exclusion of Negroes. Prior to the McCarran Act, about 1,000 Negroes immigrated annually from Jamaica under the British quota; the act now reduces that number by 90 per cent.

The Displaced Persons Act of 1948, which brought 393,500 DP's to America, was a commendable gesture of asylum to the homeless. But it turned out to be magnanimity with strings attached: Congress made these refugees quota immigrants. Because they came from countries with annual quotas too small to accommodate so many at once, the act provided that they "borrow" quotas from future allotments. Therefore, the quota numbers granted the DP's were charged to the future quotas of their countries, to be deducted at the rate of 50 per cent a year. In other words, the yearly quotas will be cut in half until the "loan" to the refugees is paid up. Thus, Poland's quota is "mortgaged" to the year 2000; Rumania's to the year 2019; Estonia's to the year 2146; little Latvia's to the year 2274. Yet, in the period from 1925 to 1952 nearly 2,500,000 quota numbers went to waste—more than six times the number of DP's admitted.

A liberal law?

Says Will Maslow, director of the American Jewish

Congress: "Fair and dispassionate scrutiny of the beginnings and development of the national origins principle and of the motives and purposes which it expresses must yield the conclusion that the national origins formula is racist in conception and operation and that it is repugnant to our national ideals."

Harmful to our economy?

Says Professor Oscar Handlin of Harvard, whose *The Uprooted* won a 1952 Pulitzer Prize: "We can and ought to take advantage of the possibility of profiting from immigration. Certainly in the past ten years we have suffered from shortages of particular kinds of labor in various parts of the country. I do not mean to argue that immigration was the only way in which these shortages could be relieved. But I would argue that immigration was a convenient, expeditious, and cheap way of doing so, and one in accord with the traditional ideals of our country."

To that, the President's Commission adds: "Immigration has made a positive contribution to our economic life. Reliable evidence indicates that immigration neither contributes to nor aggravates unemployment . . . In the period of unrestricted immigration, the volume rose during prosperity but rapidly disappeared in times of depression when it would have contributed to unemployment."

Experts in the problem say our economy—always dynamic, always expanding—needs immigration to strengthen the labor force. We were caught short during the last World War—and still suffer an acute manpower shortage —because of our rigid immigration policy. During the last war men were pulled off the farms to build planes and ships, Southern Negroes were shifted to the cities of the North and West, Puerto Ricans and other West Indians were imported by the hundreds of thousands, and 5,000,000 women were called to the war plants. The shortage appears worse today. About 1,500,000 more women are on jobs than at the wartime peak of 1944. The situation has been aggravated by a drop of 2,000,000 people in the age group of ten to nineteen years, in the decade ending 1950. (It is estimated an immigrant of eighteen years is worth $10,000—the cost of rearing him in the United States.)

Edward Corsi, Industrial Commissioner of New York, told the President's Commission: "We are suffering from a very great labor shortage in this state both on the farm and in the factory." He said there were 350,000 unfilled nonagricultural jobs and 4,500 unfilled farm jobs in New York state alone.

Former Secretary of Labor Maurice J. Tobin testified: "As an over-all conclusion, I would say that the future holds for us a continuing tight situation, so far as manpower resources are concerned, and that we may safely gauge our immigration policies accordingly."

But what of all those "unassimilables"?

Says Professor Philip M. Hauser of the University of Chicago: "No other nation in the history of man has provided as inspiring and convincing a demonstration of the fact that any people of any ethnic origin or race can do what any other people in the world can do; and can achieve the highest possible standards of social, economic, and political existence if provided with the opportunity to do so. In re-enacting the quota system of 1924 into Public Law 414, we have in fact closed our minds and our hearts to one of the truly great contributions that the United States has made to human knowledge and to the cause of world citizenship."

You will hear the argument that the United States cannot be expected to shoulder the burden of solving the world's over-population problems. Quite so; the United States is not expected to. This nation, as any nation, has a right to select its future citizens. Immigrants must be screened to keep out the habitual criminal, the insane, the diseased, the subversive. The point is: We need a fair, just, sensible selective process—not a formula that is itself subversive, being based on religious and racial prejudices promoted by political demagogues for their own expedient purposes.

Rabbi Abba Hillel Silver of The Temple, Cleveland, had a thought on this: "Racial conceits and pretensions have frequently been used by the forces of privilege, darkness, and reaction—and the great religions of mankind have always warned mankind against them. Paul declared in a magnificent summary of the Judeo-Christian tradition on the subject of race: 'The God that made the world and all nations therein . . . hath made of one blood all nature and men to dwell on the face of the whole earth.' "

Rabbi Silver goes on to quote a Jewish sage: "God created only one Adam, in order that in the future no man shall be warranted in saying, 'I come from better stock than you do.' "

Chapter

5   Among other things, Public Law 414 invests consular underlings with absolute power; allows immigration officials to imprison aliens indefinitely without a hearing; holds a Damoclean threat of deportation over the head of every alien in our midst; sets up a second-class citizenry, and creates an atmosphere conducive to corruption.

Mr. Walter, co-author of the act, condemns the vigorous opposition to it as stemming from two sources: 1) the Communists and their dupes; 2) those who have not read the law. Mr. Walter, obviously not a Red, and not a dupe in that sense, must be unaware that the Communists heartily favor this law.

The McCarran Act tossed to the Reds a jewel beyond their most extravagant daydreams. Without a honeyed whisper in a cloakroom ear, without so much as the expenditure of a lobbying dime, the Communists got what they would want.

This was a law that makes the Hitlerian doctrine of Aryan supremacy our national policy. This was a law that embeds two all-powerful police states in the structure of our democratic government. This was a law that—so contrary to the American way—clothes little men in the raiment of the medieval despot, pits race against race, cruelly tears families asunder, insults our good-neighbor nations, rewards alien veterans of our wars with banishment, flouts the Constitution as if it were a municipal parking ordinance. This was a law that stirs up dissension at home and alienates our friends abroad.

What better could suit the evil purposes of the Kremlin? We hand Russia on a platter a choice propaganda bird, done to a turn—all gratis. Choice it is, because, for once in the Cold War, the Soviets need fabricate no lies when they exploit against us the rather fantastic occurrences taking place under the McCarran Act.

Granted that the Communists, of their own brazen accord, could not have lobbied this law into being. But once it was enacted, how best could they keep it on the books? By opposing it—and the more blatantly the Reds oppose, the more tenaciously the act's sponsors cling to it. For such is the devious party line: discredit the thing you want, support the thing you don't want. This has been the traceable pattern over the years.

Naturally, the Communists and their dupes oppose this law.

But others oppose it too, for more creditable reasons.

President Dwight D. Eisenhower time and again has called for revision of the law. During his election campaign, he told a Newark audience, "The McCarran Immigration Law must be rewritten. A better law must be written that will strike an intelligent, unbigoted balance between the immigration welfare of America and the prayerful hopes of the unhappy and the oppressed."

It is inconceivable that even Senator McCarthy, in his wildest grab for a headline. would dare label Mr. Eisenhower a pinko, or the dupe of pinkos.

Former President Harry S. Truman, also no Communist, in plain-spoken messages to Congress vetoed both the McCarran-Walter Act and its precursor, the Internal Security Act of 1950, often dubbed the first McCarran Act.

Among the national organizations that have spoken out against the provisions and consequences of this law are the National Council of Churches of Christ, the National Catholic Welfare Conference, the National Lutheran Council, the Union of American Hebrew Congregations, the Synagogue of America, the National Council of Catholic Women, the American Friends Service Committee, the AFL, the CIO, the International Ladies Garment Workers Union, the Amalgamated Clothing Workers of America, the Jewish Labor Council, the National Association for the Advancement of Colored People, the American Civil Liberties Union, the American Bar Association, the Association of Immigration and Nationality Lawyers, the American Association for the Advancement of Science, the American Council of Learned Societies, the Anti-Defamation League of B'nai B'rith, the American Jewish Congress, the National Council of Jewish Women, the Young Women's Christian Association, the General Federation of Women's Clubs.

Forceful arguments for a complete revamping of the act came from the President's Commission in its magnificent report, *Whom We Shall Welcome,* prepared under the direction of Harry N. Rosenfield, executive director of the Commission, and issued January 1, 1953.

Senator McCarran, taking a cue from a senatorial colleague, hastened to brand the report as "a rehash of the 'line' that was parroted by the radical left-wing clique in Congress." This "clique" which had opposed the law included such men as Senators Green, Saltonstall, Douglas, Kefauver, McMahon, Lehman, Moody, Humphrey and Sparkman.

Senator McCarran charged that the Commission was trying to raise "a wave of racial and religious bigotry" and had resorted to "the same Big Lie catch-phrase technique" of the Communist *Daily Worker* in its attack on the law. "It is a tragic fact," said the Senator, "that the out-and-out Reds have ready colleagues in this fight: the 'pinks,' the well-meaning but misguided 'liberals' and the demagogues who would auction the interests of America for alleged minority bloc votes. . . . The act is very tough on Communists, as it is on criminals and other subversives, and that is why they are squealing."

Chairman Philip B. Perlman of the President's Commission replied: "The Senator cannot make a reasoned defense of an act which embodies so much discrimination and prejudice. So he ignores the facts and makes unfounded insinuations and smears against those who disagree with him."

Mr. Perlman pointed to the fact that of 634 persons who appeared at the Commission hearings, only eighty-seven expressed approval of the act. And many of these eighty-seven expressions of approval were identical arguments offered in various cities by representatives of the same national organizations, such as the Daughters of the American Revolution.

Senator McCarran's remark about the "parroted line" appears all the more irresponsible in view of the caliber of the men who served on the Commission: Chairman Perlman, former Solicitor General of the United States; Earl G. Harrison of Pennsylvania, former U. S. Commissioner of Immigration and Naturalization, and former dean of the University of Pennsylvania's Law School; Monsignor John O'Grady of Washington, D. C., secretary of the National Conference of Catholic Charities; Reverend Thaddeus F. Gullixson of Minnesota, president of the Lutheran Theological Seminary of St. Paul and chairman of the Minnesota Displaced Persons Commission; Clarence E. Pickett of Pennsylvania, honorary secretary of the American Friends Service Committee; Adrian S. Fisher of Tennessee, legal adviser to the State Department, former general counsel of the Atomic Energy Commission and solicitor of the Department of Commerce, and Thomas G. Finucane of Maryland, chairman of the Board of Immigration Appeals, Department of Justice.

So much for that.

Now let us examine Mr. Walter's second claim—that only those people oppose the law who have not read it. If that were so, then at least 159,000,000 Americans must be opposed to the McCarran Act. To say that ten out of a million Americans have read the act would be a pretty conservative estimate. The staggering truth is that ninety-nine out of a hundred who might try to read it would have difficulty understanding it. Very likely, before the ordinary reader reached Section 243 (b) (2) he would be strapped up in a strait jacket.

The professed aim of the law's sponsors was to codify earlier statutes, to clarify and simplify our immigration laws. Yet the McCarran Act is so incredibly complex, such a tangled mass of obscurities, obsolete phrases and double-talk that even a person trained to breeze through legal verbiage has a hard go making much sense out of it.

Max Rheinstein, professor of law at the University of Chicago, told the President's Commission: "I would like to say one additional word as a lawyer. It may also look a bit petty and perhaps insignificant, but I don't think it is, and that refers to the technical defects. To put it more popularly, nobody can understand it at all. It is so complicated. There are sections in it which are twelve pages long.

"May I invite your attention to Section 202 which I think nobody can understand until he has read it twelve times. I have read it now thirteen times, and now I *think* I understand it. If and when a revision of this law is undertaken, I hope to goodness somebody will be called in as an expert in English. As it stands now, it is an abomination on the English language. It is even worse than the Code of Internal Revenue."

Section 202, dealing with the determination of the quota to which an immigrant is chargeable, has only five sub-sections and eleven sub-subsections, but all of them are masterpieces in obscurity. For instance, sub-subsection

(3) of subsection (a) states: "An alien born in the United States shall be considered as having been born in the country of which he is a citizen or subject, or if he is not a citizen or subject of any country, then in the last foreign country in which he had his residence as determined by the consular officer."

At first blush, and even at many later blushes, this somehow gives the impression that an alien born in the United States (aren't *natives* born here?) could have taken up residence in some other country before his birth. How could a consular officer determine *that?*

But if you think that is puzzling, test your perception on sub-section (5) of subsection (a) of Section 202: "Other than as specified in paragraphs (1), (2) and (3) of this subsection, or as defined in paragraphs (27) (A), (27) (B), (27) (D), (27) (E), (27) (F), (and) (27) (G) of section 101 (a), any alien who is attributable by as much as one-half of his ancestry to a people or peoples indigenous to the Asia-Pacific triangle defined in subsection (b) of this section, shall be chargeable to a quota as specified in that subsection; *Provided,* That the spouse and child of an alien defined in section 101 (a) (27) (C), if accompanying or following to join him, shall be classified under section 101 (a) (27) (C), notwithstanding the provisions of subsection (b) of this section."

Perhaps this was what former Attorney General James P. McGranery had in mind when he told the Commission that the act failed to achieve the "simplicity of arrangement to be expected of an exhaustive codification," that it might lead to "further complications of administration," and that it contained needless and intricate cross-references made more confusing by an unwieldy numbering system.

"This criticism goes to the act as a whole," Mr. McGranery said. "I could discuss extensively the ambiguities and defects of numerous specific sections . . ."

Despite all this, when President Eisenhower pointed out certain glaring faults and suggested that Congress revise the act, Mr. Walter had the temerity to say the President had "joined the army of critics who have failed to read the act they criticize."

Has Mr. Walter read the act?

Some doubt was cast on that point last March when Mr. Walter was in Los Angeles for sessions of the House Un-American Activities Committee. At that time the Los Angeles *Daily News* was trying to halt the deportation of Rosa Orozco, wife of a veteran. Mr. Walter told a television audience there were ways and means of keeping her in the United States, but he did not amplify.

Boyd H. Reynolds, an immigration counselor, wired the Congressman: "I would like to know what ways and means there are for keeping Mrs. Orozco here."

In his reply, published in the *News,* Mr. Walter said Mrs. Orozco was "under a complete misapprehension." He declared there was a specific provision (which he did not identify) in the act that made it unnecessary for Mexican nationals living here to return to Mexico in order to adjust their immigration status.

Commented Herman R. Landon, director of immigration for the Los Angeles district: "If there's such a provision in there, I don't know about it. We've tried to explore everything under the sun and are trying to be as sympathetic as possible and still comply with the law."

As a matter of fact, the law permits suspension of deportation, while an alien irons out his immigration troubles, to everyone except our neighbors. It *specifically denies* that privilege to most categories of deportable Mexicans, Canadians and Cubans.

Equally incomprehensible are numerous other provisions. In Public Law 283, passed by the 82nd Congress, a section fixes criminal penalties for transporting aliens unlawfully into the United States or harboring them. One Federal Court ruled this section was unconstitutional and void for vagueness; another Federal Court, acquitting a defendant, commented upon the vagueness of the language. Yet, two years later, and in the face of these decisions, the McCarran Act reproduced that paragraph exactly in Section 274 (a).

Section 287 empowers any immigration officer to interrogate without a warrant "any alien or person believed to be an alien as to his right to be or remain in the United States." The San Francisco *Chronicle* contended this "invites abuse by overweening immigration officials."

The same section empowers immigration officers to enter without a warrant "private lands, but not dwellings," within twenty-five miles of the border. However, one midnight in May, 1953, armed immigration officers conducted a raid on the Marysville, California, Chinatown, almost a thousand miles from the Mexican border. The Chinese Six Companies of San Francisco, an association of Chinese-American citizens, which protested the raid, described it through counsel as a "Russian-styled violation of citizens' rights." Newspaper accounts related that the officers blocked all roads into and out of town and prevented any Chinese—citizen or not—from leaving town. Then they stopped Chinese on the streets, entered homes, herded everybody into two buildings and held them incommunicado for five hours. Three Chinese were booked for illegal entry into the United States.

Under the McCarran Act, a prospective immigrant need not necessarily be *convicted* of a crime to be denied a visa. He is considered ineligible for a visa if he simply admits "committing acts which constitute the essential elements" of a crime. That clause has lawyers baffled. And if it baffles lawyers, how can a consular underling, untutored in the law, be expected to interpret the clause justly and fairly?

Equally vague—and condemned as unjustifiable by any standards of decency—is the clause empowering the attorney general to suspend the deportation of an alien if, in his opinion, it would result "in exceptional and extremely unusual hardship" to the alien or his family. Is human misery to be standardized like olives—small, medium, large, extreme, extremely extreme, colossal misery? How would you classify the heartache of a mother torn from her babies? Public Law 414, by sanctioning it, considers such anguish neither exceptional nor extremely unusual.

An alien can be deported "if it appears to the satisfaction of the attorney general that he or she has failed or refused to fulfill his or her marital agreement." This provision prompted former Senator Blair Moody, Michigan Democrat, to ask in the Senate: "What earthly business is that of the attorney general?" And Senator Hubert A. Humphrey, Minnesota Democrat, expressed the possibility that the law might become "a sort of congressional Kinsey report."

As if the vague language of the act itself were not enough, the Immigration Service has set up its own regulations to compound the confusion. These regulations often go beyond the law.

One regulation provides that if a hearing officer finds you statutorily eligible for voluntary departure, to spare the stigma of deportation, but the officer does not exercise the discretion *for reasons of his own,* you have no right of appeal. But if the hearing officer finds you do not qualify under the law for voluntary departure, you have the right of appeal. In other words, if you are *eligible,* you can't appeal; if you are *not* eligible, you can appeal. To lawyers too, this doesn't add up.

These are only a few of the things that have stirred up opposition to Public Law 414. Yet Senator McCarran claimed that the President's objections to it "affect only insignificant matters and are not sound . . . not a single objection has any force or effect." Mr. Walter went further and said none of the faults deplored by Mr. Eisenhower actually exist in the act.

A tacit admission that they do exist came from Representative Patrick J. Hillings, Republican of California, a member of the Senate-House Immigration "Watchdog"

Committee. He conceded: "Some of these objections can be met by regulations. It's more a matter of administration than bad legislation."

Let us examine some of the injustices Mr. Walter claims do not exist, and let us see how these objections are being met by administration.

Chapter

6

You are a pro-NATO, anti-Communist
Frenchman living in the northern part of France. You and
your bride honeymooned in America years ago, and you
were then so enchanted with this country that you vowed
to come back some day. That day has arrived, and you go
to the American consulate in the nearest city and apply for
a visa. You are wearing a beret.

The minor official assigned to the visa section in this
consulate has an aversion to berets. He doesn't look good
in one himself. He takes your application and curtly tells
you he will notify you later. You go home and wait.

There is an investigation. Military attachés at the Embassy are asked for a file on you. Snoopers poke into your
past, query neighbors about your habits, deportment,
financial affairs, affiliations, what thoughts you have ever
expressed.

You don't know it, but the investigation shows that you
are A-1, O.K., a great guy, without a stain.

Months later you are summoned to the consulate. The
underling glances up at you and shudders. You are still

wearing that beret. Your application for a visa is denied.

But why, monsieur?

You get a blank stare, then a terse reminder that the interview is at an end.

Baffled, you put on your fatal beret and go home.

Your chances of visiting again the land you fell in love with are dead as a Christmas goose. There is no one else you can appeal to. The consul general is not empowered to help you. Even the Secretary of State literally cannot do a thing. This underling's word is final. And he need give no reason, other than perhaps his unamplified conclusion that granting you a visa would be contrary to the best interests of the United States.

Incredible? But that's the law. The McCarran Act, Section 221 (g), specifically states that no visa shall be issued to an alien *if it appears to the consular officer* that such alien is ineligible for a visa. And there is no appeal. The consular officer may be an individual embittered by the minor post he holds after years in the foreign service, or he may be a young fellow totally unfamiliar with the character of the people he judges and untrained to weigh evidence.

The law confers upon this consular officer the absolute, life-and-death powers of a medieval king, for it can mean just that, life or death, to a refugee denied asylum in his flight from tyranny. The McCarran Act also clothes this official in the spangled aura of a professional crystal gazer, a calling outlawed in most American cities. Thus he is authorized to say to an alien who desires to emigrate to America and establish a business, "I predict that ten years from now there may be a depression, you will become bankrupt and be forced to go on relief, so I cannot grant you a visa." Or he may legally tell a man, "I expect you may some day grow feeble-minded and become a public charge, so I cannot grant you a visa."

Fantastic? Not if you apply the simple test lawyers use to determine whether any law invites abuse—not what *is* done under it, but what *may* be done. Even so, what *is* done under this segment of Public Law 414 defies belief.

Granting of such despotic power flabbergasts legal experts, as evidenced in testimony before the President's Commission. Louis J. Jaffe, professor of administrative law of the Harvard Law School, thus expressed his amazement:

"If you look through the whole body of the law, you will find that it is almost unprecedented that a power of such vast dimensions is granted without any review whatsoever. We have searched in vain for anything comparable to it. It has come to be a premise of our whole administration of justice that no one man should have an absolute power which cannot be reviewed anywhere.

"It is not only that this is absolute power. It is that it is uncoordinated power. It is contrary to the correct principles of administration to allow to a great number of men spread all over the globe to make the policy of the United States without any power of coordination and control in the upper hierarchy."

But then, Congressman Hillings of California says it is more a matter of administration than bad legislation. So let us see how it works out in actual practice.

Voluntary exile is the wrenching decision that confronts Forrest R. Nelson, a native-born American. He is an electronics expert engaged in highly important work for the United States Navy, but he may have to forsake that contribution to the nation's security and take up residence in some other country—in order to live with his wife.

For almost two years, at the cost of thousands of dollars, Nelson has been trying to get his wife into the United States. But so far he has been as hapless and frustrated as a man battling a concrete wall with his bare fists.

The beauteous Mrs. Nelson was born Ilda Petracchi in Alexandria, Egypt, descendant of ancient Italian and French aristocratic families. She holds two graduate degrees from the University of Paris and three degrees from the University of Berlin.

In 1927 she married Rolf Redwitz, kin of the Bavarian poet, Oskar Baron von Redwitz, and the same year accepted appointment as an associate professor at the University of Berlin. Two years later, in 1929, she became a full professor, with life tenure, of Egyptology and Islamic culture. In addition to her academic work, she achieved fame in Germany as a radio lecturer.

She was dismissed from the university in 1938 for refusal to join the Nazi Party. She taught languages for the next two years at the Academy of Stuttgart, then was accused and dismissed as an anti-Nazi. Along with her ten-year-old son, Kurt, she was sentenced to hard labor in a German munitions factory, and later to digging shelters in the hills. She stood the ordeal for three years before suffering a physical breakdown. Her husband, also an anti-Nazi, was impressed into the German army and killed in combat against the Russians in 1945.

Ilda Petracchi Redwitz Nelson is listed as Blue Booklet member No. 221 of "the persecuted people and prisoners of the Nazi system" and an honorary member of the *Comité Sanitaire Suisse,* a similar organization in Switzerland.

After the war she served for a year as interpreter for the director of the Office of Economics, U. S. Military Government in Germany. Then, with her young son, she returned to Italy where she engaged for a time in International Refugee Organization work before establishing her own language school at Genoa. In January of 1952 she and Kurt, then eighteen, came to Mexico on the Sidarma Line vessel *Andrea Gritti.* And that same month a romance that had begun in Europe led to the marriage of Ilda Redwitz and Nelson at Tijuana, with her son as a witness.

Nelson immediately requested nonquota status for his bride, as the wife of an American citizen. The U. S. Immigration Service said okay, but the vice-consul at Tijuana said no, because she had arrived in "territory contiguous to the United States on a non-signatory line." A non-signatory steamship or air line is one that has not entered into an agreement with the attorney general to permit inspection of passengers—an arbitrary provision of the law that penalizes the passengers even though they may qualify otherwise to enter the United States legally. That meant she would have to wait in Mexico two years to become eligible for entry into this country. However, her Mexican visa was good for only six months.

At the expiration of her visa, the vice-consul at Tijuana suggested that she go to Cuba, which was not then considered contiguous territory. The vice-consul assured Mrs. Nelson that her papers were all in order and that a visa would be issued promptly. She flew to Havana. Her file followed, but certain records were mysteriously missing.

Furthermore, word came from the Immigration Service that the Nelsons were not actually married. A clerk had failed to record the marriage. Nelson was even accused of trying to smuggle an alien into the United States. He flew to Havana, and they were remarried. The Immigration Service once more gave its blessing.

But not the American consul at Havana. He ordered a new investigation, including duplicates of papers obtainable only in Europe, which Nelson did obtain at a great outlay of time and money. By now, Mrs. Nelson's temporary Cuban visa had expired. She was granted an extension at the request of the Italian consul in Havana. Still the American consulate stalled. When her extended visa ran out, the consul advised her that all the necessary documents required by law were in his possession, and the required investigation completed, but he wanted to check a little further. Just hang on, he urged, and a visa would be forthcoming in a matter of days.

But the Cuban authorities refused to grant a further stay. She flew back to Tijuana, and in six months will likely have to try Cuba again. The consul at Havana, where the visa is still being processed, is quite nice about it. Every few months, in response to repeated queries, he reassures Mrs. Nelson's attorney that "her application has received, and will continue to receive, every consideration consistent with the immigration laws and regulations."

Strangely enough, Nelson had no difficulty bringing his stepson, Kurt, into the United States on a student visa, and the boy is now studying at a California college. Mrs. Nelson's brother, Raymond Petracchi, a Los Angeles city employee, has been a United States citizen for more than twenty years. Yet for nearly two years Mrs. Nelson has been shuttling back and forth between Tijuana and Havana, knocking in vain at our golden door.

That is why Forrest Nelson, who traces his own ancestry straight back to the Mayflower, is faced with a bitter choice: to give up his wife, or give up his country.

Even American citizens who travel abroad are not immune. Under the arbitrary powers granted consular officers, such tourists may suddenly find themselves exiles. All because a presidential proclamation of 1941—issued for wartime security reasons, but still in effect—decreed that no citizen could leave or enter the country without a passport.

Say you arrive in Rome on your European tour. Your personal effects, including your passport, are destroyed in a hotel fire. You go to the American consulate to get a new passport, but a consular officer doesn't think you are a citizen of the United States and rejects your claim. Any carrier that may bring you back home is subject to confiscation of aircraft or vessel, plus prosecution for a felony. You run into quite an expense burning up the trans-

Atlantic cables for the proof of citizenship that may make the consular officer change his mind.

Before the McCarran Act went into effect, such claimants had recourse to the courts. But even then bureaucracy often dogged them. In many such cases the State Department has refused to provide documentation, although it was a defendant in a court proceeding and the agency that rejected the original claim of citizenship. The State Department justified its refusal on this round-robin argument: such a documentation would permit the citizen to come to the United States and fight his case.

One Federal Court upheld the State Department, saying it didn't have to issue a travel document to permit the citizen to come here unless it wanted to. Three other Federal Courts ruled that the State Department must issue such a document under due process. Thus the citizen's chances of proceeding to the United States to pursue his claim of citizenship depended on the judicial district in which the court action was taken.

Public Law 414 neatly sidestepped that problem. It simply decreed that a person claiming United States citizenship wasn't entitled to anything, unless a consular officer abroad so decided. Under the new law, there is no judicial relief whatever.

Take the case of the Sing brothers. Gum Sing and Foon Sing were born in a small village in South China, the sons of Wong Sing, an American citizen. Gum, twenty-two, had lived in Hong Kong for five years; Foon, eighteen, had just joined his brother there.

Both applied for an American passport. The consular

official at Hong Kong questioned the brothers separately and at great length to determine their kinship to each other and to Wong Sing. Their testimony was identical in all particulars and agreed with the deposition of the father, taken in the United States. That is, it was identical in all details except one—the position of a washstand in the living room of their home in the Chinese village.

Gum Sing, who had not been home in five years, recalled that the washstand stood on the north side of the room. Foon Sing, recently arrived in Hong Kong, said it stood on the south side. The consular official rejected their claim of derivative citizenship on that discrepancy. And so the Sing brothers cannot come to the United States to live with their American father.

"The very fact of the discrepancy tends to show the genuineness of their testimony," says the father's counsel, Boyd H. Reynolds of Los Angeles. "It is commonly taken for granted that we all can't agree on everything. Three witnesses to an auto accident may give three different versions of it."

It also happens that the washstand in question was a *movable* washstand.

What immigration lawyers dub the "Chic Sale decision" sets off the Yee case as a bit unusual. Yee Suey Keung, fifteen, and Yee Suey On, thirteen, the sons of Yee Wing Art, an American citizen, were born in a small Chinese village. They applied at Hong Kong in March, 1951, for a travel document to come to the United States as derivative citizens. In June, 1953, more than two years later, the consular officer refused them a travel document on this ground: "Applicant Yee Suey Keung testified that the village toilet accommodated two people at one time, his applicant brother stated that the village toilet accommodated only one person."

The father's attorney, Harold D. Kline of San Francisco, in an appeal brief to the State Department's Panel Board, argued: "The discrepancy as to the capacity of the outdoor plumbing in the home village . . . is completely absurd and frivolous in nature since it has no significance in determining the principal question at issue. It would be just as relevant to the issue of citizenship to inquire as to what an applicant had for breakfast on a specified date six months ago."

Chapter

7   At last you've got a visa. It's been a long, long wait, perhaps years. The consul likely knows more than you do about your past, present and probable future, your financial status, the clubs you belong to, the people you've talked to lately. And you've passed rigid medical examinations: you are not leprous, tubercular, alcoholic, psychotic, or idiotic.

You had a little farm on the outskirts of an Italian town, or you were an Austrian school teacher, or a Dutch merchant, or an Estonian engineer who fled the Communist tyranny and spent the last few years in a crowded refugee camp. You've sold the farm, given up the teaching job or liquidated the business, and packed your possessions. You sail with your family to the land of new opportunity. Or if you are the refugee, hounded and persecuted over the years, you depart for America bolstered by visions of storybook freedom and the chance to prove your worth— an individual under God and laws that proclaim equality and justice for all; no longer an automaton, a cog in a police state.

Whoever you are, you are coming to America with a visa

acquired after an ordeal. There were, for instance, the questions. Answer Yes or No, are you now or have you ever been: a prostitute, or a procurer? a habitual drunkard? a polygamist? feeble-minded? unfaithful to your wife (or husband, as the case may be)?

Of course, we do not want undesirables—they *must* be kept out. But surely a method of inquiry could be devised that would be less of an affront to respectable people.

A University of California scientist, who came from a European country a few years ago, offered a typical comment on the present screening process: "At first, I was startled by these questions—was I an imbecile, or a pimp, or a bigamist? Then I was rather amused, but I couldn't help wondering why America should embarrass visitors in this way. It seemed so ridiculous. If I were a pimp, I most certainly wouldn't admit it."

But never mind. You endured such crassness because of your great desire to see or live in America, and now you are approaching the beautiful land—Mei-kuo, the beautiful land, is the Chinese word for America. In your pocket is the visa, a welcome to the United States. And ahead— see the great lady?—stands the Statue of Liberty, torch held high. Perhaps a lump rises in your throat, tears of joy and gratitude very possibly drift down your cheeks, as the ship slides past the statue.

But wait, you haven't landed yet. The State Department gave you the works abroad.

Now the Department of Justice takes over. To be exact, the Immigration Service of that department, with its motto: Guardian of the Gates. One attitude behind that motto was betrayed by the annoyance of a retired immigration official of Texas, in reply to a critic of the service: "We don't want those foreigners over here. It was all right fifty or a hundred years ago, maybe, but we're out of the horse-and-buggy days."

So the golden door may not swing open for you, after all. You may be hauled off to detention quarters. At the port of New York it is famed Ellis Island. Across the continent, at San Francisco, aliens are held in barracks-like rooms with double-barred windows on the upper floors of a downtown skyscraper: the twelfth floor for men, the thirteenth floor for women and children. Civic groups have decried the use of this federal office building as a place to imprison men, women and children—even babies—for months, occasionally years.

You, who have never been in jail, never had a blemish on your record, may languish in detention indefinitely, without a specified charge against you, without a hearing. Why? Simply because an immigration inspector suspects you. Of what? He won't say, and he doesn't have to say.

Argyle R. Mackey, Commissioner of Immigration and Naturalization, insists such is not the case. He says all aliens thus excluded are informed of the reason: "Their entry would be deemed prejudicial to the interests of the United States."

That is not a reason, but a *conclusion*. Suppose a cop grabbed you as you walked along the street minding your own business. He hustled you off to jail. You would demand, and rightfully: "Why am I being held here?" And the cop would reply, "Because you are a menace to society." If a cop did that, you would scream to high heaven.

Yet such is the treatment often accorded to the immigrant arriving at an American port with a valid visa. He is given no reason for detention over unconscionably long periods. *Why* would his entry be deemed prejudicial to the interests of the United States? Therein lies the reason. And without such a specification of charges, legal experts say he is denied due process of law.

Under the American concept of justice a man accused is clothed in the presumption of innocence until proven guilty. He must be confronted by his accuser, and given the right to answer the accusation.

The Immigration Service substitutes its own theory of justice: A man accused is guilty, and the burden is upon him to prove his innocence. It may be only a suspicion, resting on the shaky ground of gossip or the word of a secret informer. Short of a hit-and-miss attempt over a million years, lawyers say a person could never prove himself innocent of a charge if he had not the faintest notion of what he was accused.

Justice Robert H. Jackson assailed this philosophy of justice in a sharp dissent warning against "police state" methods, in the case of Ellen Knauff, the German war bride detained on Ellis Island for three years without a hearing and without disclosure of the "confidential information" against her. The Supreme Court held, four to three, that it had no right to intervene.

Said Justice Jackson: "The menace to the security of this country, be it great as it may, from this girl's admission is as nothing compared to the menace to free institutions inherent in procedures of this pattern . . . The plea that evidence of guilt must be secret is abhorrent to free men, because it provides a cloak for the malevolent, the misinformed, the meddlesome, and the corrupt to play the role of informer undetected and uncorrected."

The immigration authorities, with congressional approval, deftly dodge all such criticism. They say the immigrant—and right now hundreds of them are being held in the downtown San Francisco skyscraper, at Ellis Island, the East Boston Detention Station, and elsewhere—has not actually landed in the United States. They say he is still an alien knocking at our door, and as such he is not entitled to any rights.

To see how this works out in actual practice, consider, for one of many examples, the plight of the Saranin family. Peter Saranin, a lay official of the Eastern Orthodox Church, preferring exile to life under the Bolsheviks, had long ago fled to China. His stepson, Alexander, represented big United States corporations in Shanghai. Alexander's pretty, vivacious wife, Elizabeth, born in Harbin of White Russian parents who had also fled the Bolshevist terror, had a married sister living in Texas.

At the end of World War II Russia offered amnesty to political exiles. The Saranins, believing, as other White Russians in China did, that the Kremlin had changed its ways, took out Soviet passports. In the event they wanted to move on, they felt this was better than being stateless.

But they stayed in Shanghai, soon became disillusioned about the Kremlin's supposed change of heart, and in 1946 they took their passports to the American consul and said,

"We want to become American citizens. Already we decide always to speak English to each other." They had a four-year wait before they got their visas, just in time to board the *General Gordon,* the last evacuation ship out of China. This was the elder Saranin's second flight from Communism.

They were seized when the vessel docked at San Francisco. Mrs. Saranin was locked up on the thirteenth floor of the skyscraper bastile; Peter and Alexander on the floor below.

"At first," Mrs. Saranin related, "they said we would be detained only a few hours, then only a few weeks, then only a few months. We never knew what they had against us. We were not Communists. We only wanted to be Americans."

After seven months the Saranins were ordered excluded. Mrs. Saranin heard about the American Civil Liberties Union, founded thirty-three years ago to defend the rights of all without distinction and listing among its national committeemen such persons as Norman Cousins, Pearl S. Buck, Professor Henry Steele Commager, Dr. Karl Menninger, Will Rogers, Jr., the Reverend Harry Emerson Fosdick. Mrs. Saranin asked an inspector about the ACLU and said she was told: "Get them and the case will go against you. They are in bad standing in Washington."

The Saranins did eventually secure a lawyer, who petitioned for a writ of habeas corpus. However, the attorney general informed the court that the Saranins were being held "on confidential information," and that was that.

A year passed, and the Saranins remained in the detention quarters, husband and wife a floor apart. There was little to do but pace, and the months dragged endlessly. Mrs. Saranin, the gay and lively young woman who had embarked on the *General Gordon* with such anticipation of a new life in America, was driven by the starchy diet, the frustration, and the perplexity of it all to the edge of a nervous collapse. At length, she begged her jailers: "We will pay our own way back to China if you will please let us out of here."

Commissioner of Immigration Mackey insists the Saranins were advised they "were free to leave at any time," but they "chose to remain." The bald fact is that no other country wants a person rejected by the United States.

In August, 1951, broken financially and spiritually, the Saranins departed for Hong Kong, en route, they said, to Russia. They had come to America full of great dreams; they had got only a glimpse of it, for fifteen months, through double-barred windows, and they left never knowing why. They sailed either to their doom at the hands of the Reds for daring to seek sanctuary in America or, more likely, to feed the insatiable Soviet propaganda mill.

Mrs. Saranin told a newspaperman on board ship the day they departed: "We heard nothing but good of America, and found nothing but bad. We've heard nothing but bad of Russia—maybe we will find a little good."

Why were Peter Saranin and his family treated so shabbily, then turned back to the Communists they had fled? What was the nature of this "confidential information" that some secret informer had furnished against them?

Were the Saranins dangerous to the security of the United States, or were they the victims of malicious gossip?

This may offer a clue: a White Russian who lived in Shanghai before the Reds took over revealed that some members of the White Russian colony were jealous of the Saranins and particularly envied Alexander's modest affluence as a representative of big American firms.

An individual need not be suspected of a Communist taint to merit detention. Some months ago a noted British pacifist, invited here to address Quaker groups, was held on Ellis Island for several weeks before newspaper headlines won his release. Immigration officials admitted there was no question of Communism or subversion involved; they simply felt his entry for the announced lectures would be "prejudicial to the interests of the United States."

Dr. and Mrs. Shen Wu-wan had a similar experience, for a slightly different reason. Dr. Shen, a Chinese scientist, had a contract to engage in research at Yale University for the United States Navy. They were seized at San Francisco and held incommunicado, and separately. This unexpected treatment made Mrs. Shen ill. When Yale and influential friends protested the humiliation, the Shens were released, after four days. The Immigration Service offered this explanation without apology: Dr. Shen's visa was "invalid" because the Navy contract was "renewable for years," without specifying any particular date.

Such tactics are not reserved solely for aliens. Citizens also suffer from the administration of our immigration laws.

Two Chinese boys came to the United States late in 1951

to press their claim of derivative citizenship as the sons of a native American. The boys, after a lengthy investigation, were given travel documents in lieu of a passport, by the American consul in Hong Kong. They were to come to San Francisco, where their father lives, but they somehow got on the wrong plane at Tokyo and landed at Seattle. The father, unaware they had taken the wrong plane, was not in Seattle to meet them.

They were detained by Immigration and later given a hearing. The hearing officer rejected the boys' claim of citizenship. One of the principal grounds for the rejection was the failure of the father to meet the plane at Seattle. The hearing officer contended that if they were actually his sons, the father would have been there to greet them.

Counsel for the father advised the hearing officer that he objected to the entire proceedings and would seek judicial redress. Before he could take the matter into court, however, he had to exhaust what administrative remedy was available—an appeal to the Board of Immigration Appeals in Washington. He appealed, in November of 1951.

Next word he heard in the matter was a cable from the boys—in Tokyo. They had been deported by plane from Seattle on February 12, 1952, immediately after the Washington board had rejected the appeal, and before the attorney was notified of the decision. The boys had been refused permission to telephone either their father or the attorney. The day after he received the cable from the deported youngsters in Tokyo, the attorney was notified of the dismissal of his appeal.

The attorney was appalled. He protested to the immigration authorities in Seattle, who admitted the summary deportation of these sons of an American citizen was "regrettable" and "unusual," but said there was nothing they could do about it. Immigration regulations specify that an attorney must be notified of any decision by the Commissioner of Immigration before any adverse action is taken, but the Seattle immigration officials held that, inasmuch as this was a decision of the Appeals Board rather than the Commissioner, the attorney was not entitled to notification.

Shocking? Quite so, but immigration investigators do worse. They wheedle "confessions" of alienage out of Chinese-American war veterans to exclude or deport them from the land of their citizenship. This has happened, a former immigration official estimates, in fifty or sixty instances, to his knowledge.

Typical is the case of Eddie Wong, servant in a Beverly Hills home. Eddie served four and a half years in the Army during World War II, more than half the time in the South Pacific. His service records listed him as a citizen of the United States. To clinch the matter, after the war Eddie petitioned the Superior Court in Los Angeles to establish the fact of birth. The court, satisfied by the evidence that Eddie was born in San Francisco on January 19, 1910, decreed him a citizen.

In the fall of 1947 Eddie obtained a passport from the State Department and went to Hong Kong. He fell in love, married, eventually became a father. He decided to return to California, get a job and an apartment, then seek entry for his wife and child, the latter an American citizen by derivation.

Eddie arrived at San Francisco by Pan American Clipper on May 31, 1949. An immigration investigator grabbed him as he descended from the plane and hauled him off to the skyscraper detention quarters in San Francisco. Eddie was held incommunicado for nine days. During that time the investigator questioned Eddie repeatedly.

"Look," the investigator would say, "you're a veteran, and so am I. I'm your friend, I want to do the right thing by you. But you're in a spot. That court decree making you a citizen was no good." He would let that sink in, then add: "But there's an easy way out. If you will just admit you were born in China, then you can naturalize as a veteran, and get this thing settled once and for all. It's very simple. Otherwise"—and the investigator would shrug —"well, you might be held here indefinitely."

Eddie trusted the investigator. He felt this was indeed a way to get the matter of citizenship permanently settled. And after nine days of this ordeal, he was ready to admit anything.

So Eddie said he was born in China and named the village of Ngow Moo Won, which he knew as the home of his ancestors.

A Board of Special Inquiry, immediately impaneled, heard his "confession" and ordered him excluded. The grounds: Eddie had no Chinese passport, nor an immigrant visa, and had admitted the crime of perjury—that is, he lied when he claimed he was a citizen in applying for the United States passport.

The Immigration Service, which ignored the court decree that Eddie was an American citizen, was itself unable to produce any evidence of Eddie's alienage or, if he were in truth an alien, any record of his entry into the United States. Apparently stricken by a mild attack of conscience, the immigration officials at San Francisco referred the matter to the Los Angeles district for an investigation in an effort to prove alienage. Statements were taken from Chinese who had once lived in the village of Ngow Moo Won, but none could identify Eddie as a person they had ever seen or known in the village. These statements, however, were not made a part of the official record.

Eddie had the right to an administrative appeal and, inasmuch as this was not a security case (no question of Communism was involved), he was released on $2500 bail. His counsel appealed first to the Commissioner of Immigration, who upheld the local board's finding, except in the matter of perjury. The Commissioner ruled that nowhere in the record had Eddie made an unequivocal admission of perjury. Next, the case was placed before the Board of Immigration Appeals. That board, which functions at the will of the attorney general, also sustained the local finding.

Eddie tried another move. He petitioned for the naturalization that the investigator had assured him would be a simple matter. But Immigration effectively blocked him here too. One section of the law states that World War II veterans, even though unlawfully in the United States at the time of their induction, can naturalize. But another section states no person can naturalize if there is a deportation proceeding against him. That let Eddie out.

The case had now dragged on for more than three years, with his wife and child still in Hong Kong. After stymieing his effort to naturalize, Immigration finally served him with a deportation warrant.

Eddie's counsel tried another step. He applied to the attorney general for relief under the Seventh Proviso of the old law. This proviso permitted an alien—if the attorney general approved—to petition for re-entry upon proof of an "unrelinquished domicile in the United States for at least seven years" prior to his departure, plus a stainless record. Counsel also pointed to the provision in the law that no alien shall be deported to a country if, in the opinion of the attorney general, he would be subject to physical harm.

"There seems no doubt," counsel argued, "that the respondent, being strongly anti-Communist, would be subjected to physical persecution, or worse, if deported to Communist China. It would indeed seem ironical that a man who has seen long and active service in the military forces of the United States during time of war, who has offered to give his life if necessary for the protection of the United States and the way of life this country represents, should be turned over to the enemies of this way of life for liquidation."

In this, and the other appeal briefs, counsel revealed the manner in which a "confession" of alienage was cajoled out of Eddie.

Despite all these pleas, Eddie, a law-abiding citizen of the United States until the immigration investigator worked him over, still faces expulsion—and an uncertain fate in Red China. The attorney general refused to grant him permission to try for re-entry under the Seventh Proviso. When immigration authorities take him into custody for deportation, his counsel plans a last, desperate move, a petition for a writ of habeas corpus. That, at the least, could be a reprieve for a few months.

Is this what Congressman Hillings of California means when he says it is more a matter of administration than bad legislation?

Chapter

8   You got past the Guardians at the Gate.
You are now lawfully in the United States. You may be an
eminent British physicist en route to Stanford for important research. You may be a Swedish dairyman, admitted for permanent residence, bound for the Wisconsin
hinterland. Or you may be a visitor touring the scenic
spots of the West. Whoever you are, wherever you go,
whatever you do, the Eye is upon you.

The Eye keeps its sharpest focus on men of learning, for
men who have acquired a great deal of knowledge are
particularly suspect. Professor Lawrence Schwartz of the
University of Nancy, France, spent wearisome months
getting a visa to deliver a paper at the International
Mathematical Congress at Harvard in September, 1950.
Upon his arrival here, Immigration placed the professor,
one of the world's most noted abstract mathematicians,
under especially strict rules of behavior. He could travel
about, but only if he gave written notification of each
change of address. He was forbidden to appear officially at
any other university, either to give or hear any lectures on

mathematics. Disheartened by it all, Professor Schwartz left the United States soon after the Harvard meeting.

An American is not even required to have a French visa to visit France.

The judges of your deportment are the immigration authorities, and they can be very strict chaperons. A Korean who had been in the United States thirty-four years was recently ordered deported because he had drifted away from the business that had originally brought him here as a so-called treaty trader. He pleaded for a stay of deportation, but was turned down, for this reason: "While the record does not establish he is a member of the Communist Party or actually a member of a Communist front organization . . . his judgment as to proper associations and activities leaves a great deal to be desired." He was eventually granted voluntary departure.

If you have been admitted for permanent residence, you must register and always carry your alien "ID" card. And if in the excitement of moving to another part of town you forget to notify the attorney general, you are subject to deportation.

Should you be convicted of a violation of any of the rules set up by the Immigration Service, you may have to pay a substantial fine or go to prison, then be deported. Regardless of whether the court imposes any penalty—regardless of whether there is a pardon or a court recommendation against deportation—the McCarran Act says you must be deported.

During your first five years in the United States, you must not come down with a lengthy, expensive illness which may put you in a public hospital for treatment. That makes you a "public charge" and subject to deportation. Formerly, an alien could escape deportation by proving the ailment that made him a public charge did not exist prior to entry. But the McCarran Act leaves the matter entirely up to the opinion of an immigration official.

The McCarran Act makes you deportable if you ever had a "purpose" to engage in activities prejudicial to the public interest. An article, "Deportation and Due Process," in the July, 1953, issue of the *Stanford Law Review* poses these questions: "What does 'purpose' mean? Is pure subjective state of mind enough? If so, what evidence would suffice to show purpose? What does 'public interest' encompass, and whose conception is to be used? Is gambling prejudicial to the public interest? Is organizing or participating in a strike?"

Say you innocently had a "purpose" to join an organization that was later designated subversive by the attorney general. You do have the defense that you joined before the organization was branded subversive. But even so, you may be deported if the attorney general decides you had *reason to believe* the outfit was subversive.

Particularly shocking to legal experts is the retroactive feature of the McCarran Act. This makes you, an alien, deportable for something you did many years ago that was not then an offense against any law. Because the McCarran Act also reaches into the future, you can never feel secure. You may do something today that is perfectly legal, yet a law may be passed in 1975 declaring such an activity to be criminal. To the born American, it will not be retroactive, but it is retroactive for you as an alien. You could *then* be deported as guilty of the innocent act you did *today*.

The McCarran Act even retroactively rescinded the five-year statute of limitations governing certain causes for deportation, in effect since 1917. Thus if your entry into the United States twenty-five years ago may have involved a purely technical error, you enjoyed an immunity from deportation for the past twenty years. You could have been naturalized before last December 24th by a simple registry process of legalizing your entry. Under Public Law 414, you are now subject to deportation. You may have an American wife and American children. Makes no difference.

As the *Stanford Law Review* points out: "At the turn of the century an alien was deportable only because he had been excludable on some ground. Today the basis for expulsion may be that the alien had no right to enter in 1900, or that for some short time after entry [in 1900] he believed in anarchy."

The Congressional Conference Report on the act stated that "the conferees have provided for a statute of limitations [as contained in the House version] in accord with humanitarian principles." But the statement referred only to what the President's Commission described as "the exceedingly narrow provision that mental disease or economic distress after entry will justify deportation at any subsequent time only if it occurred within five years after entry." Under the McCarran Act, deportation proceedings for any other cause can be brought at any time.

Criminal prosecution for a violation of the immigration law is outlawed after three years, but a deportation action for the same offense—even for a mistake that offends no criminal law—can be brought forty or fifty years later. After so long a time it can be impossible to gather witnesses and evidence to make a defense.

Carl Friedrich, professor of government at Harvard, assailed this retroactive legislation in testimony before the President's Commission: "I think it is subversive of all good order and law. The Nazis did it, and the Communists do it, and it is an uncivilized, undemocratic, illiberal method to say that because I now feel differently about something that was done ten years ago than I felt ten years ago, I will now decree that what was done ten years ago was then a crime or a criminal act. This is slightly unacceptable for any kind of legislation."

Actually, these retroactive features represent a form of *ex post facto* law, forbidden in criminal statutes by the Constitution. However, the Supreme Court has held that deportation is a civil matter, not a criminal punishment. And so the Constitutional ban on *ex post facto* laws does not hold here.

Still, for a civil matter, deportation can exact a terrible penalty—exile, among other hardships. Judge Augustus Hand labeled exile "a dreadful punishment, abandoned by the common consent of all civilized people."

These are only a few ways and means of deporting an alien. Unjust as they seem, an even worse feature is that deportation is often left to the sole discretion of an individual in the Justice Department, some minor official or the top man himself, the attorney general.

Remarking on this before the President's Commission, former Senator Benton warned that "absolute discretion, like corruption, can mark the beginning of the end of liberty." He counted forty-one places in the act "where power to exclude or deport is dependent on the opinion of a consul, or upon the opinion of the attorney general." He went on: "There are sixty additional places in the bill (Public Law 414) where deportation or exclusion, or other overt actions in regard to aliens, or even naturalized citizens, is dependent on the facts being established 'to the satisfaction of the consul' or the 'satisfaction of the attorney general.'"

Senator Humphrey, who co-authored the Humphrey-Lehman bill, a liberalized immigration law that was rejected in 1952, said it was "unthinkable that we should vest in the attorney general so much power over human beings . . . We do not give the State Department or the Justice Department that much power over a can of sardines imported into this country."

But then, Congressman Hillings of California says it is only a matter of administration. Let us see.

Gustavs Ildimars Freibergs escaped from Latvia under fire from Communist troops and ultimately reached America in 1947 on a visitor's visa. He tried to get his status changed to permanent residence in order to apply for citizenship, but that was denied because he would not be able to get an immigration quota number. Latvia's quota was exhausted and will be for some time. (The Displaced Persons program "mortgaged" Latvia's quota to the year 2274.)

Freibergs' temporary visa was twice extended, and during this period he was drafted. Before his induction he married an American girl, and they established a home in Los Angeles. He served six months in Korea, was rotated back to the States and discharged. Soon afterward Immigration ordered him deported to Latvia—because, while he was off fighting in Korea, his visitor's visa had expired. His story got into the Los Angeles *Times,* and a special bill was introduced in Congress to halt his deportation. Some 1500 such bills have been introduced. It's surprising how much congressional relief should be sought from an Act of Congress.

Gilberto Benitez-Villalba is a 52-year-old Los Angeles grocer. His sensitive features, rimless glasses and trim mustache give him a professional air. He is married to a United States citizen and one of his five children, Jesus, is a disabled veteran of World War II.

Benitez came up from Mexico with his parents in 1912. Nine years later, at the age of twenty, he was convicted of burglary in Texas. He served fourteen months, with time off for good behavior, and was then deported. In 1926, with the attorney general's permission, he returned on an immigrant visa.

Of that long-ago crime, Benitez says ruefully, "I was young and foolish, and I've regretted it ever since."

He had good reason to regret it when he applied for naturalization in September, 1949. An immigration investigator checked his record, then issued a warrant of arrest. He said Benitez' authorized re-entry twenty-four years earlier was unlawful because, *in the investigator's opinion,* he was not entitled to it.

Benitez retained counsel and applied for the privilege of voluntary departure under the Seventh Proviso which would entitle him to come back on another visa, regardless of the legality of the 1926 entry, because he had had a good record for at least seven years. After debating the matter for two years, Immigration rejected his plea for voluntary departure and ordered him deported. This would mean he could never return to the United States. His family, all American citizens, would have to become exiles in order to be with him—including, of course, the son disabled fighting for his native United States.

Counsel appealed. Benitez was finally granted the voluntary departure relief he had so desperately sought, just two months before the McCarran Act went into effect. It was a tight squeeze. Because the investigator held that Benitez was technically not entitled to the 1926 re-entry, the McCarran Act, by retroactively rescinding the five-year statute of limitations for such technical violations, would have made deportation mandatory—forever barring him from coming back. Some lawyers hold that, because of the vagueness of the McCarran Act's definition of what constitutes good moral character, Benitez' one-time conviction of a crime—even though it had happened thirty-two years ago, and even though he had atoned for it—might have gone against him, had voluntary departure not been granted in time.

Even so, when granted voluntary departure, there was a time limit of ninety days placed on his return, or he would be permanently barred. Benitez made it back on January 17, 1953, just one day before the deadline.

And there is the ordeal of this Rumanian family: Ion Maniu, a chemist; his wife, Carmen, a former teacher; their son, Nicolae, 9, and their daughter, Magda, 6.

The elder Manius, then in Rumania, applied in 1947 for student visas for advanced study at an American university. Maniu got his visa in time to enroll for that fall semester. Mrs. Maniu's visa was held up for no announced reason.

When Rumania became a Soviet satellite early in 1948, Mrs. Maniu and the children were trapped. It took her a year to talk her way out of Rumania, bringing her children here on a visitor's visa.

Meanwhile, Maniu applied for permanent residence as a Displaced Person on the ground that it would be unsafe for him to return to Rumania, now that it was under Red domination. His petition was approved by Immigration and eventually, late in 1952, by Congress.

Mrs. Maniu, whose visitor's visa had been extended, then sought DP status for herself and children. She had no counsel at the hearing on her application, and the hearing officer questioned her sharply as to her reasons for leaving Rumania. She explained that her husband feared to return to Rumania and therefore the only way they could live together as a family would be to establish residence elsewhere.

Her application for DP status was denied. She and her

children were ordered deported. Reasoned the hearing officer: "Since she, by her own admission, did not intend to return to Rumania with her children, and since they did not have a visa to a country beyond the United States, the conclusion is warranted that they intended to reside in this country permanently. This intention renders their entry into the United States on a visitor's visa unlawful entry."

Actually, Mrs. Maniu entered the United States legally enough. But the hearing officer, as so often happens, confused *desire* with *intent*. She said her intent was to seek a temporary haven in the United States and, if regulations forbade staying, to go on to a South American country with her family. When her husband obtained DP status, she was told she would be within her rights—and she was—to apply for similar standing.

She retained an attorney, who obtained a reopening of the case. Again the hearing officer denied her application, but this time on the ground she was not a stateless person—she could return to Rumania if she wished. He reached the decision despite the fact that her husband had already been granted permanent residence here as a Displaced Person.

The attorney appealed, and the Commissioner of Immigration granted her DP status. Now Congress must approve, which may take several years. Meanwhile, her fate remains uncertain. Congress can disapprove. In that event Maniu, who has sunk roots here, will have to pull them up. They speak English and Rumanian; if Congress turns her down, they may have to go to a country whose language they do not know.

That is another wrinkle in the McCarran Act—you can be deported to a totally strange country, providing, of course, that country will accept you.

Chapter

9 A young Chinese woman arrived in Los Angeles from Hong Kong in January of 1952 on a visitor's visa. She fell in love with a Chinese-American citizen and they were married the following October.

Wedding bells rang too soon for this bride. She should have held off another three months. By marrying within a year after her arrival in the United States, she ran afoul of the McCarran Act. She cannot stay here while she irons out her immigration difficulties. She must go all the way to Hong Kong, and then she can come back as the wife of an American citizen.

This fantastic bit of nonsense highlights a feature of Public Law 414 known as suspension of deportation, which permits an alien under certain conditions to remain here while he settles his account with Immigration. This is an aspect of the law that is particularly notable for absurdities.

For one thing, it insults our good neighbors. An alien subject to deportation can in most instances apply for a halt in proceedings if he hailed originally from anywhere in the world except our next-door nations. If an alien at odds with Immigration comes from Canada, Mexico, Cuba, or any adjacent island, he is entitled to little or no consideration. Out he goes, forthwith.

Even for those from the eligible continents the McCarran Act, while endeavoring, as the Congressional conferees put it, to be "humanitarian," actually makes this worthwhile procedure so unwieldy it's hardly workable. Formerly, it was quite a simple matter, but Public Law 414, as it did in so many places, substituted an intricate machinery.

Under the old law, any alien could qualify for this administrative relief if he had already lived in the United States seven years or if deporting him would cause economic hardship to his family, no matter how short his residence here. The new law requires, for suspension of deportation, a continuous "physical presence" of from five to ten years, depending on the case. For an alien with an American family, there must be proof that his deportation would, "in the opinion of the attorney general, result in exceptional and extremely unusual hardship" to his kin.

Here we have the degrees of misery again. The Senate Committee report made it clear that such remedy as suspension of deportation "should be available only in the very limited category of cases in which the deportation of the alien would be unconscionable." The report went on: "Hardship, or even unusual hardship to the alien or his spouse, parent or child is not sufficient to justify suspension of deportation."

The President's Commission quoted a witness: "Rarely has there been a balder statement of a national policy to be cruel."

Equally indefensible is the regulation prescribed by the Immigration Service, over and above the law, that these matters may be decided on the basis of a secret and confidential policy. A suspension may be denied for reasons withheld from the alien or his counsel. This practice of determining the fate of a man and his family in secrecy is foreign to our standards of due process.

The ten-year residence requirement applies indiscriminately to former subversives, criminals, prostitutes and persons whose entry long ago may have been a mere technical violation of the immigration law. In all cases, the alien must prove he was a person of good moral character for ten years up to the moment he applied for suspension. Yet the law's definition of good moral character is highly restrictive and vague. For example, he must not be "one who during such period has committed adultery." Even the Immigration Service complained about the inadequacy of this definition.

Moreover, only an alien who entered the United States before June 27, 1950, may be granted a stay of deportation if a final order of deportation has been issued. Thus, the date of such an order arbitrarily controls an alien's right to qualify for a delay.

In all events, Congress has the final word. Under the previous law, suspension of deportation became final if Congress failed to disapprove it. The new act makes it a bit more complicated. In some cases, failure of Congress to pass an *unfavorable* resolution makes the suspension final; in other cases, failure of Congress to pass a *favorable* resolution makes it final.

This insistence by Congress on the last say in such matters is considered by many authorities as an encroachment upon the powers of the executive branch of the government, contrary to the intent of the drafters of the Constitution. Commented the President's Commission: "This is wrong in principle and bad in practice. It is no more the function of Congress to pass upon individual cases involving suspension of deportation than it would be to pass upon the issuance of individual visas, or for that matter upon the custom inspection of an individual alien's baggage. One searches in vain for a comparable example of intermingling of executive and legislative authority."

The joker of this whole machinery, set up ostensibly to help an alien adjust his immigration status with ease, is this: Often enough, a deportation is carried out as a technicality merely to comply with some minor quirk in the law, and the victim is then qualified to return as a permanent resident, once he had made the long journey to his native land. In some instances, he would even be entitled to preferential treatment for a visa by virtue of having a citizen wife or children; yet he must suffer the heartache of a disruption in his family life, and the financial burden of a trip abroad—simply to come right back. The alien may easily lose his job while he is away, and his family may have to go on county relief. And he is always subject to the whims and delays of a consular officer overseas.

Thousands of Mexicans in California and the Southwest face deportation for clerical errors in the record of entry, or for entering without proper inspection, or for long-forgotten youthful escapades. These are not the so-called "wetbacks," the seasoned farm laborers who sneak across the border to work the crops, but residents of the United States for years, many with American-born families. Most of them cannot escape deportation, once it is ordered—except by special dispensation from Congress—because, as explained earlier, the McCarran Act specifically denies the common categories of deportable Mexicans (and Canadians, Cubans, Haitians, Bermudans, Jamaicans, and natives of other "adjacent islands") any right to adjust their difficulties here.

These cases come to official attention in sundry ways: when an alien applies for naturalization; when, under the new law, he registers his address every January—and if a lawfully resident alien forgets to do so one year, he is subject to prosecution and deportation; through black-mailing informers; if the police happen to pick him up on a traffic ticket; by roundups in communities and raids on farm bunkhouses.

Sponsors of Public Law 414 evidently justified their lack of provision for natives of our neighboring nations on the theory that all such an alien had to do was cross the border into Canada or Mexico, or hop down to Jamaica, pick up a nonquota visa as easily as he might buy a souvenir, then return, a legally admitted alien ready for citizenship. And Immigration people still insist that is so—just take the family along, make it a day's outing, a picnic across the border.

But an American consular officer at Tijuana told Counsellor Boyd H. Reynolds of Los Angeles: "The deported alien is in for a bitter disappointment. He must go to the end of the line. The fact that he has an American family makes no difference. Getting clearance to re-enter usually takes from six to eight months."

And often longer. This is not theory; this is reality.

Sometimes the story of an alien's plight gets into the newspapers. Then Congress, goaded by the publicity, will consider a "private" bill to soften the hardship it condones in Public Law 414.

Consider, for example, the case of Rosa Orozco, wife of Jose Orozco, a native of Los Angeles. Before Jose was inducted into the Army in 1946, he took a vacation trip to Guadalajara. There he met Rosa, a pretty, dark-eyed Mexican girl. They fell in love.

Jose returned home, went into the Army, and on his first furlough drove to Guadalajara and married Rosa. He brought her back to Los Angeles to live with his parents while he went to Korea to serve with the occupation forces.

It didn't occur to Jose that his bride would need a visa. After all, he was an American citizen, and she was his wife. Nor did it enter Rosa's innocent mind that she was doing anything wrong by crossing the border without inspection. After all, she was coming with her husband, and he was proudly wearing the uniform of an American soldier.

While Jose was in Korea their first child, Rosa Linda, was born. One day, talking to a friend who had had experience with the immigration authorities, Rosa was astonished to discover that she was unlawfully in the land of her husband—by coming here without a visa.

In all honesty she went straight to the immigration office

and confessed her error. She was immediately served with a warrant of arrest. Bewildered, she sought the help of Immigration Counsellor Reynolds, who applied for suspension of deportation, at that time permissible for Mexicans. Immigration eventually approved the petition, and it was sent on to Congress for a final okay. Like hundreds of similar petitions, hers lay in Congress for several years—until it was too late. The McCarran Act went into effect, abolishing stays of deportation for most of our next-door aliens. Rosa Orozco was ordered out of the country.

She and her husband, Jose, were panic-stricken. They now had four children—Rosa Linda, five; Richard, three; Alberto, one, and Edward, four months.

By rare good fortune for the Orozcos, Joseph Saldana, a reporter on the Los Angeles *Daily News,* learned of their plight and wrote a story. This came to the attention of Congressman Chet Holifield of Los Angeles, who introduced a private bill in Congress to grant Rosa Orozco permanent residence. There was some hope it would go through. At least, it had the immediate effect of halting deportation until Congress could act.

What of the thousands of such cases throughout the Southwest, from Texas to California, that do not reach the press?

The Orozco story was given a big play in the Mexico City newspapers. One clipping, with the words INHUMANA LEY (inhuman law) blazoned in the headline, was tacked on the bulletin board outside the Foreign Office in the Mexican capital. Beneath it was scrawled: "This is what our friends think of us."

Chapter

10   Alice Mays Sullivan, a Canadian, lived in a Florida city with her husband Harry, a United States citizen. One day she and a friend were shopping in a department store. They stopped at a bargain counter and looked over the purses on sale at $1.98. Unconsciously Mrs. Sullivan walked away with one and was arrested at the door.

Next day she appeared in court, without an attorney. She says: "There was a crowd in the court, and I was so embarrassed and confused. The judge asked me several questions and my mind was in such a whirl I answered yes, yes. He fined me $25. I paid it quickly and left. All I wanted was to get out of there."

A year ago she went to Canada to visit her parents— briefly, she thought. She is still there. She can never return to her home and husband—forever barred, because of that $1.98 bag.

The United States consul said her only remedy would be to secure a pardon. But it so happened she had pleaded guilty to a violation of a municipal law. And Florida cannot issue a pardon for a conviction under a municipal ordinance.

Florida authorities suggested an alternative relief—that she return, withdraw the old plea, stand trial and win acquittal. But she can't return to purge her record, because her record forbids her re-entry.

If she slipped across the border and won the right to re-entry by an acquittal, she would be deported for unlawful entry. And if deported, she would be exactly where she is today—in an unresolvable dilemma.

The real irony is the fact that Mrs. Sullivan was not deportable for picking up that bargain purse. She could even have become a naturalized citizen, if she hadn't gone to Canada on a visit. She was simply trapped—as many another alien has been—by the re-entry doctrine of the McCarran Act.

Under Section 223 (b) of the law, the attorney general may, in his discretion, issue a re-entry permit, valid for one year, to an alien lawfully admitted for permanent residence (she was) who desires to visit abroad and return to the United States, if the application is made in good faith (hers was), and if the alien's proposed departure from the United States would not be contrary to the interests of the United States (hers wasn't).

Mrs. Sullivan complied with all these requirements. Then, bearing a re-entry permit, she went holidaying to Canada, blithely expecting the United States Government to live up to its side of the bargain in equally good faith.

But there's a joker in this section of the McCarran Act too. A re-entry permit is actually not a permit to re-enter.

The very next subsection, 223 (c), says such permit "may be used by the alien in making one or more *applications* for re-entry into the United States." (Italics mine.) And a following subsection makes it even plainer, that a permit "shall have no effect under the immigration laws except to show that the alien to whom it was issued is returning from a temporary visit abroad."

Thus, a resident alien who drives across the bridge at Detroit to see a British movie in Windsor, or flies to Havana for the week-end, or takes a business trip to London, is subject to the same threat of exclusion as a newcomer—even though he has a re-entry permit. Let's say an alien, here more than five years, becomes tubercular and goes to Arizona, leaving his business and family in Chicago. He is not deportable for having contracted TB in the United States. Some fine Sunday he drives down to Nogales, across the border, just for the afternoon. He cannot come back, because an alien suffering from TB is not admissible.

Charlie Barnes was four years old when his parents brought him from Canada in 1906. He grew up in Chicago. In 1947, deciding to migrate West, he drove out with his family, including two small girls. At El Paso, as most tourists do, the Barnes went over to Juarez for a Mexican meal. Barnes was not one to tarry on a motor trip, so they were back across the border and on the highway within two hours.

Last February he applied for citizenship. Had he ever been out of the United States since his parents brought him here? Barnes replied no, then remembered the brief visit to Juarez five years earlier, and said: "Oh, yes, once, in 1947, when we were driving out West. We went across to Juarez, just for lunch."

"Did you have a Border Crossing Identification Card or a re-entry permit?" the inspector asked.

"Why, no," said Barnes. "We were only over there a couple hours, if that long. Just for lunch, like I said."

A warrant of arrest was immediately issued on the ground he was unlawfully in the United States. As a Canadian, he was not entitled to suspension of deportation while he adjusted the matter. He had to go to Canada to re-enter on an immigrant visa—a journey that might take, not a day for a round trip, but months, depending on the consular officer. It did take months. He lost his job. His family went on relief.

All this impresses our friends from overseas. Item: Edmund W. Tipping, then city editor and now the featured columnist on the big Melbourne, Australia, *Herald,* was awarded by the Carnegie Corporation an Associate Nieman Fellowship to study at Harvard during the academic year of 1951-52. His wife and three children came with him. During the Christmas holidays they planned to visit relatives in Canada. Says Tipping:

"Just in case of visa trouble, I checked in with the immigration people in Boston to make sure. They said I'd be O.K.—just to call at the United States Embassy in Ottawa and announce my presence. So, when we were ready to return from Ottawa, I did—and what a shock! The consul said I couldn't re-enter the United States unless I had a letter from Harvard saying I was needed back there. He resolutely refused to speak to the Harvard counsellor for foreign students on the phone.

"The certificate they gave me in Boston turned out to be quite invalid once one left the United States. Because of this business—and to complicate things, Western Union was on strike—we had to wait around in Ottawa till the letter turned up.

"Even with the letter I had to take my place in the immigrants' queue at Montreal before they'd give me the opportunity to produce it. I had to hang around for four hours—with Marg and the kids waiting in the car, fighting off the traffic cops."

Max Rheinstein, the University of Chicago law professor, spoke of this to the President's Commission: "It is very hard for people abroad to understand why anybody who has once resided in the United States, as an alien, who before he left the United States has applied for and obtained a permit of re-entry—why he is stopped at the port of entry and may have to spend days or weeks, and there have even been cases of years spent at Ellis Island. Those cases are simply not understood abroad."

Ignatz Mezei seems doomed to spend the rest of his natural life on Ellis Island.

Mezei was a lawful and law-abiding resident of Buffalo, New York, for a quarter of a century. In May of 1948 he sailed for Europe on what proved to be a fruitless, fateful journey to visit his dying mother in Rumania. Denied entry to that country, he had to remain in Hungary for a year and a half because of "difficulty in securing an exit permit." Finally, granted permission to leave and possessing a *bona fide* immigrant visa (his re-entry permit had expired), he headed back to his wife and home in Buffalo.

He arrived in New York on February 9, 1950. He was taken to Ellis Island. An immigration official ordered him excluded, and the exclusion order was made permanent the following May by the attorney general on the "basis of information of a confidential nature, the disclosure of which would be prejudicial to the public interest."

Mezei discovered he had no place else to go. All other countries, apparently taking a cue from the United States, refused him sanctuary. He was never given a hearing, and no charge was placed against him. After he had been held twenty-one months on Ellis Island, a Federal Court considered further detention unjustifiable unless there were affirmative proof of his danger to the country. The attorney general refused to divulge the confidential information, even *in camera,* and the court ordered Mezei released. He went on to his home in Buffalo.

The Government appealed to the Supreme Court, which ruled, five to four, that Mezei had to be locked up again on Ellis Island.

Justice Black, a dissenter, held that Mezei's continued confinement without a hearing violated due process of law. He contended: "No society is free where government makes one person's liberty depend upon the arbitrary will of another . . . Mezei should not be deprived of his liberty indefinitely except as the result of a fair open court hearing in which evidence is appraised by the court, not by the prosecutor."

The Government claimed that Mezei's transfer from

ship to Ellis Island was "for safekeeping" and that he was "not being detained in the usual sense, but is in custody solely to prevent him from gaining entry into the United States in violation of law. He is free to depart from the United States to any country of his choice." (He had no choice. He tried Great Britain, France, and a dozen South American countries, to no avail.)

Justice Jackson, who also authored a dissenting opinion, said:

> "Government counsel ingeniously argued that Ellis Island is his 'refuge' whence he is free to take leave in any direction except west. That might mean freedom, if only he were an amphibian! Realistically, this man is incarcerated by a combination of forces which keeps him as effectually as a prison, the dominant and proximate of these forces being the United States immigration authority. It overworks legal fiction to say that one is free in law when by the commonest of common sense he is bound . . .
>
> "Quite unconsciously, I am sure, the Government's theory of custody for 'safekeeping' without disclosure to the victim of charges, evidence, informers or reasons, even in an administrative proceeding, has unmistakable overtones of the 'protective custody' of the Nazis . . .
>
> "I have not been one to discount the Communist evil. But my apprehensions about the security of our form of government are about equally aroused by those who refuse to recognize the dangers of Communism and those who will not see danger in anything else.
>
> "Congress has ample power to determine whom we will admit to our shores and by what means it will effectuate its exclusion policy. The only limitation is that it may not do so by authorizing United States officers to take

the life, the liberty or the property of an alien who has come within our jurisdiction without due process of law, and that means he must meet a fair hearing with fair notice of the charges.

"It is inconceivable to me that this measure of simple justice and fair dealing would menace the security of this country. No one can make me believe that we are that far gone."

Chapter

11 To most people, strategic Alaska is part
of the United States. The McCarran Act holds two views
on the matter: it is, and it isn't. This peculiar logic applies
also to our other territories and possessions.

Public Law 414 does not say outright that Alaska, for
instance, is a foreign country. In fact, it states just the
opposite. Yet an American citizen who takes a holiday
cruise to Nome may have a hard time getting back, for
reasons other than meteorologic.

Say a New Zealander, after the usual, meticulous screening, was admitted to Hawaii ten years ago for permanent
residence. He could even become a naturalized citizen of
the United States. But if, before naturalizing, he were to
take a vacation trip to San Francisco, he would be treated
exactly as if he were arriving from New Zealand, where he
hasn't touched foot in a decade.

Ever since 1917 the immigration laws have required that
an alien, even though a lawful resident of an insular territory or possession, be subjected to the same exclusionary
restrictions at our continental gates as if he were coming

fresh from a foreign country. The McCarran Act extended this policy to Alaska for the first time.

The law specifically defines Alaska, Hawaii, Puerto Rico, the Virgin Islands and Guam as *part of the United States,* then, by placing such restrictions on visitors from these possessions, catalogues our American territories as foreign lands. Citizens as well as aliens may run into trouble at this mainland barrier. For the act also defines the term "alien" to mean "any person applying for admission to the United States as a citizen or national of the United States."

In view of that, if you are planning a voyage to Alaska next summer, or to Hawaii this winter, you might do well to take along proof of your citizenship. John P. Boyd, district director of immigration at Seattle, the first port of entry from Alaska, issued just such a warning through the Seattle *Times:* "Everyone coming in from Alaska must be able to satisfy the examiner that he is an American citizen."

Perhaps the hardest hit by this new restriction are the alien fishermen—lawful residents of the United States—who migrate from West Coast seaports to Alaska for the annual salmon run. Although by the McCarran Act's own definition they are simply moving from one part of the United States to another, they hesitate to take a chance under the new law for fear they might not be able to come home after the salmon season.

Contractors engaged in vital defense construction in Alaska also find this feature of Public Law 414 somewhat of a handicap in recruitment of workers. The A.B.C. Roofing & Siding, Inc., of Seattle, submitted this protest to the President's Commission two months before the effective date of the McCarran Act: "Conditions are hard enough for contractors in Alaska without having the added burden of clearance through immigration procedures. We sincerely feel that this is the silliest act which has ever been enacted and should be repealed before it has a chance to become a law."

The absurdity of it all was pointed out by Earl N. Ohmer, president of the Petersburg, Alaska, Chamber of Commerce, who said Alaskans generally were "much disturbed" by the law, adding: "By all means we are strongly in favor of picking up anyone or any group who might be contrary to the welfare of the United States, but we cannot see how this is rightly applied to Alaska. Such people, if they are in Alaska, must have come from the United States. If they are checked up here and found wanting, then that would mean they would have to stay in Alaska, which is one of our very important defense fronts."

Congressman Walter has stated categorically that no government agency opposed the act he helped conceive. Here is what James P. Davis, director of the Office of Territories, Department of the Interior, told the President's Commission:

"We are deeply disturbed by the provisions of the new act, Section 212 (d) (7), which imposes restrictions upon the travel of aliens from Territories to the continental United States. We believe that no useful purpose can be served by requiring such a second examination. This requirement appears to us to be burdensome, valueless and discriminatory. An alien residing in Alaska, which is a part of the United States as defined in the immigration law, should be as free to travel to Seattle as an alien residing in Seattle is now free to travel to Spokane. Each is traveling from and to points within the United States."

However, immigration authorities cannot determine whether an alien has met the requirements of this section until they first determine whether he *is* an alien, or simply "any person" seeking to enter from Alaska as a citizen. Thus, all without distinction are subject to a brisk going-over.

"Introducing such complications to travel between the Territories and the continental United States can produce no salutary consequences," Davis declared. "Normal intercourse with the Territories will be hindered, and this in turn may be expected to affect adversely the rapidity of Territorial development."

The McCarran Act does far worse by the citizenry of this country. It sets up two classes of citizenship—first and second. It makes the naturalized citizen inferior to the native-born.

John Marshall, the great Chief Justice, said in 1824: "A naturalized citizen becomes a member of society, possessing all the rights of a native citizen, and standing, in the view of the Constitution, on the footing of a native. The Constitution does not authorize Congress to enlarge or abridge these rights."

The McCarran Act tossed that historic view out the window.

Formerly, fraud or illegality in obtaining citizenship

were the grounds for losing it. And certainly a person is not entitled to citizenship acquired in such a manner. However, the McCarran Act discards that definite formula and presumes a man commits fraud if his naturalization was procured "by concealment of a material fact or by willful misrepresentation."

Thus, a naturalized citizen must be stripped of his citizenship if within ten years after his naturalization—normally, fifteen years after his entry into the United States—he is convicted of contempt in refusing to testify before a congressional committee as to his subversive activities, if any. Other citizens can do that and get off with a jail sentence; but a naturalized citizen gets jailed, denaturalized and deported. Refusal to testify under these circumstances may not be desirable, but a citizen should be a citizen for a' that. It happens, as lawyers point out, that this refusal has no bearing on provable fraud in the original naturalization.

The naturalized citizen also presumably commits fraud by concealing a material fact if within five years after naturalization he joins a group the attorney general later may consider subversive. He runs the grave risk of losing his cherished citizenship and being deported as well. The risk is all the greater in view of the difficulty of distinguishing a real patriotic organization from a Communist front group in these days when the Red outfits carry such high-sounding patriotic names to catch the unwary. The innocent may be ensnared by something that sounds and seems like a cultural society, or even a garden club. A good example is the Civil Rights Congress, a Communist front organization obviously so named to confuse it in the public mind with the highly respectable American Civil Liberties Union.

If the naturalized citizen within five years after naturalization takes up permanent residence abroad, Public Law 414 says that is *prima facie* evidence, sufficient to revoke citizenship, that he concealed or willfully misrepresented such travel plans when he obtained his citizenship.

Legal authorities declare it is extremely difficult to prove the presumption of fraud in all such cases. For one thing, what may be today of so little concern that the naturalization examiner would not even think of questioning you about it, may become, in a different political climate many years later, the "concealment of a material fact." Example: You become naturalized, and next year you join a consumers co-operative; twenty years from now that co-operative may be found to be subversive; therefore, it may be presumed you concealed a material fact when you acquired your citizenship by joining the co-operative within five years.

On the question of denaturalization, Congressman Walter once again reveals his unawareness of the contents of the law to which he lent his name. In a magazine article he stated: "It [the act] also provides that in every case involving the revocation of citizenship the courts—and only the courts—can make the decision."

That falls short of the whole truth. It is true so far as Section 340 goes, but Mr. Walter passes up Section 352 (a). In this section no presumption is even necessary: loss of citizenship is automatic, without a court decision, by mere residence abroad. The first-class citizen can remain abroad as long as he pleases, with no strings attached. The second-class citizen had better watch out.

This particular millstone was picked up from the Immigration Act of 1940. Since 1907 the law had considered a naturalized citizen's residence abroad only as a presumption of abandonment, and the individual could regain his status of citizen by the simple act of returning to the United States, at any time. The Act of 1940 changed that. It abolished the mere presumption and made loss of citizenship absolute.

The McCarran Act carries on, and somewhat confuses the matter. Under Section 340, if the naturalized citizen takes up residence abroad within five years of his naturalization, he loses his citizenship, by court decision. Section 352 says if he goes abroad *any time* within twenty-five years and remains three years in the land of his birth, or five years anywhere else, he's no longer an American— and no court action is necessary. This latter feature draws especial criticism because loss of nationality results from a legislative decree, rather than from the judgment of the court that originally granted the citizenship.

And look what the McCarran Act does to the aliens who fought in America's wars. Veterans of the Spanish-American War and both World Wars can naturalize, even if they entered the United States illegally. (Korean veterans must have been lawfully admitted.) However, there's again a joker. One section of the law permits the veteran to naturalize, but another section bars the naturalization of any person against whom a deportation warrant is outstanding. Therefore, if an unlawfully entered veteran petitions for citizenship, Immigration can halt the proceedings—and has done so on numerous occasions—by the simple process of issuing a warrant of arrest, charging him with unlawful entry.

Naturalized veterans too can lose their citizenship by comparatively brief absence from the United States. Dan Martin, a Canadian who won United States citizenship by fighting with our forces in World War II, was summoned to his former Canadian home by an illness, and subsequent death, in the family. The situation required that he and his wife, a native of the United States, remain there for several years. Upon their return, Martin was detained by immigration authorities in Detroit for five hours, then told he had forfeited his citizenship by his absence of two years (then the time limit), was fingerprinted and escorted back across the border. Martin says: "When they gave me this 'Indian' gift of citizenship, they didn't tell me there was a catch to it."

Another new feature of the McCarran Act deals with loss of American citizenship by so-called dual nationals. Some countries, such as the United States and Switzerland, confer the nationality of parents on children wherever they are born. Thus, a child born in the United States of Swiss aliens would be a citizen of both the United States and Switzerland; or if he were born in Switzerland of American parents, he would be a national of both countries. A native-born American in such a situation loses his American birthright if, after his twenty-second birthday, he spends three consecutive years in Switzerland and claims the benefits of that nationality, unless he takes an oath of allegiance before an American diplomatic officer. No court action is required. The President's Commission feels there should be no limitation on the purposes for which a native American can reside abroad, provided he chooses to retain his United States citzenship.

Under the McCarran Act a judicial decree of citizenship can be set aside by an administrative process. Say an alien, ordered deported, wins a suspension of that order, and Congress approves. He is now lawfully admitted for permanent residence and becomes a naturalized citizen. But if, within five years after he acquired the lawful residence standing, it should "appear to the satisfaction of the attorney general that the person was not in fact eligible for such adjustment of status, the attorney general shall rescind the action . . ." That automatically denaturalizes the citizen and puts him right back where he was—facing deportation, after he had enjoyed all the rights of citizenship. The American Civil Liberties Union attacks this provision as representing "punishment for acts not committed by the person punished."

The attorney general can also authorize denaturalization simply by publishing notice, if the individual is out of the United States or out of the judicial district where he last had his residence, even though the citizen's whereabouts may be known or can be ascertained to permit personal service. He may also cancel citizenship by written notice sent to a person's last known address. Exercising remarkable restraint, Professors Louis J. Jaffe and Henry M. Hart,

Jr., of the Harvard Law School assailed such notices as "grossly inadequate."

Without a statute of limitations, an action to denaturalize may be brought at any time. Therefore, the second-class citizen can never feel secure. Worse, circumstances often change over the years, and the lapse of time may cause unwarranted injury to innocent victims.

The gravity of such penalty was touched upon in a recent Supreme Court decision (Schneiderman v. United States; 320 U.S. 118,122): "In its consequence [denaturalization] is more serious than a taking of one's property, or the imposition of a fine or other penalty. For it is safe to assert that nowhere in the world today is the right of citizenship of greater worth to an individual than it is in this country."

The late Supreme Court Justice Wiley B. Rutledge warned of the inherent danger of denaturalization without proper safeguards (Schneiderman v. United States: 118,-167): "No citizen with such a threat hanging over his head could be free. If he belonged to 'off-color' organizations or held too radical or, perhaps, too reactionary views for some segment of the judicial palate, when his admission took place, he could not open his mouth without fear his words would be held against him. For whatever he might say or whatever any such organization might advocate he could be hauled forth at any time to show 'continuity' of belief from the day of his admission, or 'concealment' at that time. Such a citizen would not be admitted to liberty. This is not citizenship. Nor is it adjudication."

The late Justice Frank Murphy contended (Baumgartner v. United States; 322 U.S. 665,679) the naturalized citizen should not be "required to imprison himself in an intellectual or spiritual strait-jacket; nor is he obliged to retain a static mental attitude."

Professor Homer C. Bishop of Washington University told the President's Commission: "[Legislation] must take in account realistic dangers due to subversives, but it cannot move us closer to those totalitarian methods which we claim to abhor. There is a far-reaching difference between 'one who is proved to be' and 'one who is thought to be.' The law must not make possible summary action by any official."

But these are not the only ways of losing American nationality. There is the considerable matter of expatriation. Some of the ten listed grounds for expatriation, such as treason or renunciation, are beyond quesion; others, arbitrary. Often enough, expatriation leaves the American stateless. An example of the less reasonable causes for loss of nationality under this section is service in foreign armies—the idealistic young Americans of Britain's famed "Eagle Squadron" before our entry into World War II, for instance, lost their United States citizenship, although the law later granted them the privilege of regaining it by naturalization.

Another example: voting in a foreign election. Americans who as dual nationals helped defeat the Communists at the Italian polls were expatriated, even though the State Department had encouraged them to vote. Public Law 414 provided that Americans expatriated for voting in the Italian elections could regain their citizenship by appearing before an American consul and swearing an oath of allegiance to the United States. Many consular officers, however, have so far ignored this provision.

Guido and Dominic Carazzi, born in the United States and taken as youngsters to Italy by their parents, applied in 1938 to the American consulate in Rome for passports to return here. A consular officer refused them passports, stating they had lost their American nationality because their parents were Italian citizens.

Guido made repeated demands through the years. In 1951 the State Department finally issued a certificate of expatriation. He retained a lawyer in the United States, who started a court action (which, incidentally, cannot be done now as the McCarran Act leaves the matter entirely up to the consular officer, without judicial recourse). When the case was set for trial, the consular official in Rome changed his mind and issued Guido a passport.

His brother, Dominic, is having a harder time. The consul urged him, at the time of the 1948 Italian election: "Go ahead and vote. Vote against the Commies." Dominic did—and the consular official now uses that as a ground for expatriation.

Andrew R. Jones is a native of Texas, where his mother, brothers and sisters live. Some years ago Jones went to Mexico and took a job with the Mexican National Railways. Recently he tried to return to Texas. He was stopped at the border by an immigration official who said Jones has lost his American nationality by working for the Mexican railroads. The official based his claim on the Mexican rule that government workers should be Mexican citizens, and the National Railways is a government operation. This is not a law but a rule, and a rule not always adhered to. Similarly, many American cities have rules that city employees should be residents of the city, but this is not always strictly followed. Jones states positively that he never voted in Mexico, never took an oath of allegiance to Mexico or committed any act that would oblige him to be a Mexican citizen. He is having a particularly difficult time returning to the land of his birth because there is no judicial appeal from the immigration officer's decision.

In its efforts to bar or expel subversives, the McCarran Act gets pretty snarled up in cross-purposes. One section of the law permits the naturalization of an ex-Red, if he has seen the error of his ways for at least ten years. However, there is that other section which says he cannot naturalize if there is a deportation action against him. So, once he applies for citizenship, an immigration officer can arrest him and start deportation proceedings. For still another section of the act says a reformed Red can be deported *at any time*—ten, twenty, thirty years after he buried the hammer and sickle.

The law gets even crazier. An honestly converted ex-pinko *in* the United States can be booted out even though he has been anti-Communist for decades. Yet a reformed Communist abroad can come *to* the United States if he has "actively opposed" Communism for five years. And even this provision slams the golden door on refugees from the Red tyranny, because how can they, escaping through a chink in the Iron Curtain, prove five years of active opposition to Communism? Certainly the Red dictators cannot be expected to furnish them with such letters of recommendation.

We spend millions on the Voice of America to encourage defection behind the Iron Curtain. When these freedom lovers heed our call and flee to the West, we turn a deaf ear on their pleas for asylum by what has been described as "this macarranizing device." Likewise, we turn a deaf ear on the plea of George Washington, who long ago urged all Americans "humbly and fervently to besiege the kind Author of these blessings . . . to render this country more and more a safe and propitious asylum for the unfortunate of other countries."

Even after a five-year wait, for proof of active opposition to the Red ideology, these refugees won't be able to make it if a consular officer decides otherwise—unless they be Basque sheepherders.

When sheep ranchers of the Nevada ranges requested these alien herdsmen, Senator McCarran, the immigrants' son whose high office depends exclusively on Nevada's handful of voters, was stumped by his own law. The earlier McCarran Act (the Internal Security Act of 1950) barred Communists and all who advocated "any other form of totalitarianism." And the Basques? Technically, Falangists all, since Generalissimo Franco had by edict swept every man, woman and child into the Falangist fold.

However, the Gentleman from Nevada got around his own act, which he lately called "the monument I have spent years in building." He simply pushed a special bill through Congress to permit the entry of 250 Basque sheep-

herders to tend the flocks of his constituents. This made
the Spaniards very angry because the importation of the
sheepherders "mortgaged" Spain's small annual quota for
some years.

But then an odd thing happened. These Basque sheepherders didn't cotton to the lonely life of Nevada's vast
open spaces. Many of them vanished from the purple sage.
By deserting their flocks they violated their immigrant
status, and thus they became aliens unlawfully in the country. Immigration investigators began scouring the nation.
They rounded up some of the derelict Basques in the
sheepless confines of Detroit, others in equally sheepless
New Orleans.

But Senator McCarran touchingly jammed another
special bill through Congress, granting lawful permanent
residence to all 250 Basques, wherever they might be. The
hunt for the strayed lambtenders was called off. And then
the Senator, with an assist from his colleagues, imported a
fresh batch of Basques—500 this time—for the Nevada
and California ranges.

When the old McCarran Act was revised into the Mc-
Carran-Walter Act, that delicate problem of the Falangists
was made less embarrassing to the Senator's fondness for
importing shepherds. The new law bars only those who
advocate Communism or "the establishment *in the United
States* of a totalitarian dictatorship." (Italics mine.)

Professor Sterling D. Spero of New York University, in
a statement submitted to the President's Commission in
behalf of the International Rescue Committee, spoke of
that new feature: "[The act] is very specific with regard to

Communists and pro-Communists, and its authors should be commended for that. It seems to us, however, that the act is rather magnanimous with regard to other totalitarians, to wit, Nazis, Fascists, Falangists, etc. . . .

"The decisive words are, of course, 'in the United States.' No present or former Nazi or Fascist or anti-Semite will admit he, or his party, advocates a totalitarian dictatorship in the United States. They all will insist that their ideology was not meant for export . . ."

That saving clause thus implies that the Nazis, for instance, despite Hitler's announced goal of a world empire that would endure for a thousand years, really didn't include the United States in that dream of conquest.

And so, for the Nazis and their ilk, there is no five-year active reform requirement.

Chapter

12 Just prior to the end of the Second World War, a young German widow brought her newborn baby home from the hospital wrapped in a hospital diaper. She was indicted for theft and a jail sentence was imposed by a Nazi court. That was enough to hold up an American visa, at least until the consul could find a way to circumvent our own law.

This incident was cited to the President's Commission by George N. Shuster, president of Hunter College and former land commissioner for Bavaria. While he qualified it as admittedly extreme, the episode nevertheless illustrates the attitude of the McCarran Act toward erstwhile violators of foreign laws, no matter how trivial the offense.

Conviction of a single crime involving moral turpitude forever bars an alien from the United States. No one, of course, wants thieves and murderers crawling up our shores. But Public Law 414 ignores the possibility that within the errant individual may lie redemption, a thought popularly expressed as "Let bygones be bygones." Instead, the law sets up a hard-fast rule: once an offender, always an offender. Makes no difference when this single crime occurred, its nature, nor the person's spotless record of reformation.

The alien must have the unblemished character of a St. Francis—but not so poor. (President Hoover's Commission on Law Enforcement reported: "In proportion to their numbers, the foreign-born commit considerably fewer crimes than the native-born.")

Was an anti-Red in a Soviet satellite prosecuted on a trumped-up charge? That often happens. The McCarran Act exempts offenses of a purely political nature, but penetrating the disguise of a Soviet conviction is almost next to impossible, particularly since the crime is judged by American standards rather than the kangaroo justice of the Iron Curtain countries.

Was a pardon issued, or clemency granted? Doesn't matter.

Was it a major crime, or a minor offense that drew only a reprimand? Still a "crime involving moral turpitude." A shivering youth may steal a pair of old socks off a line, or a desperate father make off with a loaf of bread to feed his hungry brood, or an impoverished student tuck a book under his coat. Our immigration law brands such people as criminals, forever more.

The cloaked political offenses in particular drew this comment from Boris M. Joffe, chairman pro tempore of the Michigan Committee on Immigration, in testimony before the President's Commission: "We have seen in America that the fight against Communism has been immeasurably aided by the activities of those who have had first-hand experience, through persecution long experienced, with the Red menace. If we are sincere in wishing to combat totalitarian Communism, it would, of course, be to our great advantage to make use of the unquestioned aid that such persons can give us.

"We are handicapped from receiving such aid by our legislation on immigration which makes it impossible for such persons to come to the United States. For example, if an individual behind the Iron Curtain attempts to slow down, to revolt passively or otherwise against his Communist masters, and as a result is sentenced by the political kangaroo courts of the Kremlin to a term in prison, and then later escapes to a part of the world from which he can make application to be admitted to the United States, the very facts of his anti-Communism preclude his being admitted to the United States because under Public Law 414 he has been convicted of a crime in his native country.

"Consider the monstrosity of legislation which would leave to the determination of Communist Hungary whether or not Cardinal Mindzenty should be allowed to emigrate to the United States—since the present masters of Hungary accused him not of a political offense—and you get some idea of the travesty on justice and Americanism that such a law provides."

The President's Commission itself asserted that America's immigration laws "should not be used to enforce totalitarian 'justice.' "

But the McCarran Act goes even further. A new and harsher provision bars an alien convicted of two or more offenses regardless of whether moral turpitude was involved, if the sentences imposed totaled more than five years. The conviction could even result from a single trial, on an indictment carrying two or more counts arising out of "a single scheme of misconduct." Nor is actual imprisonment required; a suspended sentence will do.

This new provision of the 1952 Act elicited these objections from the President's Commission:

It reiterates the philosophy that there can be no rehabilitation where an alien has once erred.

It does not require an alien to be convicted of what are regarded as crimes, as distinguished from minor infractions. Conviction for any offense or violation of law is sufficient—walking on the grass; smoking in an unauthorized place; acts of juvenile delinquency; providing religious education to children in Iron Curtain countries; listening to the Voice of America—convictions for these offenses would be sufficient to bar the alien.

It ignores the fact that there are varying systems of justice in all countries. Courts in some countries may impose long terms of imprisonment and then suspend sentence or grant liberal parole; in other countries the courts may impose short sentences but require them to be served. Thus two aliens from different countries, although convicted of similar offenses, in the former case may be barred from entering the United States while in the latter case would be admitted; yet the alien barred might be as desirable as the other, in terms of American interests and welfare.

(An identical provision applies to aliens in the United States. An alien is deportable if found guilty under an indictment carrying several counts arising out of a single transaction, even though the offense occurred many years after his entry and even though the court did not consider it serious enough to impose a prison term. This, too, drew the commission's fire.)

Among the outstanding objectors to the two-conviction clause of the McCarran Act, and whose views were subscribed to by the President's Commission, were two top labor men.

Walter Reuther, president of the CIO, testified: "Workers who protest speedups behind the Iron Curtain, who sabotage Red war production, who organize free trade unions such as our own, are criminals in the lands under Red domination. If caught in these acts they become criminals in the eyes of the United States and are forever unable to come to our shores."

Boris Shishkin, speaking in behalf of the AFL, said: "The 1952 law, in effect, accepts Nazi and Communist laws and the decisions of Nazi and Communist police officials and courts as the basis for excluding refugees from totalitarian countries. There can be no justification for such a provision. The law should be changed so that the principles of our own law and our own system of government should be the criteria used in determining whether to admit or exclude aliens."

Despite Congressman Walter's claim that no government agency opposed his act, former Attorney General McGranery deplored various features of the law, among them this very provision that penalizes aliens subjected to phony charges. He said:

". . . Totalitarian countries consistently mask religious,

racial, and political persecutions as criminal prosecutions
. . . The practical problem of enforcement is that many
aliens from Iron Curtain countries undoubtedly contend
they were convicted of 'crimes' when no crime has been
committed and their sole offense was being politically
opposed to those in power.

"It will be impossible to determine the truth or falsity
of such claims. Trustworthy investigation to establish the
truth or falsity cannot be made in the countries involved.
Hence, I believe, there should be some clarification by
statute of the nebulous middle ground between crimes and
political offenses."

This two-offense travesty isn't all. Incredible indeed is
the provision that bars an alien if he admits acts "consti-
tuting the essential elements" of a crime. He has not been
convicted of a crime. He doesn't even admit committing
any crime. He simply reveals acts that, in the opinion of
some administrative officer, constitute "essential elements"
that could be a crime. Just what these "essential elements"
might be or mean has legal experts stumped.

Legal experts are particularly disturbed by the fact that
the alien's hypothetical acts are not weighed and adjudged
by a criminal court. The alien, in effect, can be convicted
of a crime he never committed, by an immigration officer
or consular officer serving in the triple roles of prosecutor,
judge and jury. And ordinarily this prosecutor-judge-jury
is a man with no legal training. Nevertheless, incompetent
as he may be to weigh facts, he can render a verdict of
guilty—where no actual crime is involved—with no pre-

ponderance of evidence necessary, nor even proof beyond a reasonable doubt.

As if this were not extravagant enough, these non-judicial jurists must decide the "essential elements" of a possible crime under foreign law. Often enough, the immigration official will not have a copy of the foreign law in question, and so he assumes that the foreign law is the same as that in the United States. Thus, he may convict an alien of a crime even though the foreign criminal authorities have not considered any crime committed, or even if a foreign court has acquitted the alien.

So the immigration authorities can operate in any code they choose—the American or the foreign, depending on what suits their purpose.

Says the President's Commission: "Immigration officials should not be given the function of balancing facts and deciding whether the facts establish guilt of a crime under foreign laws. The provision of the 1952 Act places an excessive burden on administrative authorities and lends itself to abuses in exacting admissions."

Still another new feature of the McCarran Act bars *forever* an alien who has in the past sought to enter through fraud and willful misrepresentation. Certainly such grounds should cause exclusion. But Public Law 414 introduces the principle of permanent exclusion and fails to take into account false statements made out of fear or to escape tyranny.

The Potsdam Conference granted Russia the power to repatriate by force all U.S.S.R. citizens displaced by the war. As a result, thousands of displaced Russians changed their nationality in an understandable effort to escape this forcible repatriation—to a firing squad or a slave-labor camp.

One of these was young Helen Shostenko, an orphan who had survived a harrowing experience—the wholesale slaughter of her family by the Communists. She came to the United States under the Displaced Persons program. Immigration authorities seized her aboard ship at New York and hustled her off to Ellis Island. There they held her prisoner for two and a half years, before admitting her to the United States. They accused her of perjury—because she had pretended to be a Latvian.

Similarly, Immigration held Nikolaj Perehud-Pogorelski, a fifty-seven-year-old Russian school teacher sponsored as a DP by the Church World Service, for fifteen months at the East Boston Detention Station, before allowing him to "land" in the United States. They accused him of perjury—because he had pretended to be Polish.

Others who likewise concealed their true nationality in a desperate flight from Communist persecution may be perpetually barred from the United States. Yet, under the McCarran Act, former Communists are not permanently barred.

Chapter

13

Congressmen, who enjoy an immunity for anything they say in Congress, often develop much immunity to anything they hear there. But on January 13, 1953, during a discussion on Public Law 414, its lesser house sponsor, Congressman Walter, shocked his colleagues.

He leveled an attack on what he called "professional Jews shedding crocodile tears for no reason whatsoever" over the McCarran Act. He claimed the only "concrete criticism" of the immigration law was that "some poor French sailors from the *Liberté* were unable to spend Christmas in New York City." Mr. Walter said he had looked into the matter and found that "there never was a finer crew of throat-slitters anywhere."

Actually, the 271 crew members of the French liner were held aboard ship on Christmas Eve, the effective date of the McCarran Act, for refusal to undergo the new screening requirement. They consisted of one admitted Red, and 270 men and women who declined on principle to answer all the questions of the screeners.

The San Francisco *Chronicle*, dismayed by Mr. Walter's startling attack, as were other newspapers over the country, characterized the Congressman's remarks as "asinine, or worse." The *Chronicle* observed that the French sailors "were held back for that refusal [to answer questions], and not for slitting throats."

Editorial writers generally considered it deplorable that a member of Congress of the United States should display such a lack of feeling for international relations as to call the crew of a French liner, or a vessel of any friendly nation, a bunch of throat-slitters. France threatened to retaliate by creating a small McCarran Act of its own, devised exclusively for American merchant seamen, which undoubtedly would have created an uproar in our congressional halls.

(It was the people of France who dug deep into their pockets and gave us the Statue of Liberty, referred to by a three-year-old of my acquaintance as the Stature of Liberty.)

If Mr. Walter had really looked into the matter he would have discovered, if he were not already aware that such a provision existed in his act, that crew members of the *Liberté*—and other foreign vessels—were subjected to a grilling such as only a prosecutor would dare pull on a known underworld character.

These men were questioned not merely about their political beliefs. They were asked such questions, in effect, as: When did they last visit a brothel? Were they planning to do any pimping while in New York?

Worse, the stewardesses on foreign liners, respectable girls in a respectable calling, were bluntly asked: Had they ever been prostitutes? During their few days in New York did they plan to engage in prostitution?

This indelicacy evoked such a storm of indignation abroad that our immigration authorities withdrew that line of questioning, at least in so far as the girls were concerned.

Collier's joined the quick journalistic response to Mr. Walter's astonishing remarks anent the critics of the act and the *Liberté* incident. An editorial in its issue of February 28, 1953, said in part:

"If Mr. Walter and Senator McCarran read their newspapers and their mail, they know that their bill has been called unwise, unfair and discriminatory by Americans, both clergy and laity, of all faiths. And for Mr. Walter to inject religious bigotry into his defense is to compound deliberately what we trust was originally an inadvertent error of legislative judgment.

"It would be a different matter if the questionnaire section of the 1952 immigration law gave promise of strengthening our defense against Communist aggression. In that case, we could run the risk of angering some of our non-Communist friends. But it doesn't. It simply creates a wholly righteous resentment in countries and governments which are members of the mutually reliant association of free nations. And it creates that resentment to no avail."

Since 1917 the immigration statutes have provided for inspection of alien seamen on foreign vessels, but the McCarran Act added unusually stringent screening requirements. The loophole, of course, is the fact that no Communist agent is going to answer truthfully the questions about his political affiliations, or his purposes for wanting to enter the United States. Indeed, a Communist agent need not go to the trouble of trying to enter in the guise of a seaman. There are other ways. For one, the Soviet diplomatic missions. For another, the 13,000 miles of United States coastline, plus the land boundaries across which came some 1,500,000 Mexican "wetbacks" last year —and how many of these might have been Reds?

The Detroit *Free Press,* in an editorial on January 22, 1953, succinctly contrasted this scrupulous culling at our ports with the ease by which multitudes scrambled across our borders: "It serves to make us look ridiculous in the eyes of the world; a nervous Nelly who grimly stands guard with a fly swatter at the screen door while the flies swarm in the open windows."

Alien seamen serving aboard American vessels have a far rougher go of it. For reasons not self-evident, the Mc-Carran Act is highly discriminatory toward these crewmen who help man our merchant fleet. A new provision empowers an immigration official, in his discretion, to prevent an alien crewman, who had signed on an American vessel and made a trip, from being paid off in an American port. The right to adjust an immigration status in the United States from temporary to permanent residence applies to all aliens, except seamen. Sea service counts as residence and physical presence in the United States for purposes of naturalization, but for no other purpose, such as getting a deportation order suspended while the alien irons out a technicality.

From as far back as 1800 seamen on American ships,

even though here illegally, could naturalize after a certain period of sea service. The McCarran Act of 1950 (Internal Security Act) abruptly cut off citizenship for sea service, unless the alien crewman had been lawfully admitted. Thousands of alien seamen who had their five years requirement filled and had applied, but had not yet formally petitioned for naturalization—and many had not yet got around to filing even an application—were left holding the bag.

A Canadian who had his required sea time and months earlier had even taken the first step of filing a preliminary application was injured in a ship accident and confined in a Seattle hospital the day the 1950 Act went into effect. This prevented him from filing the formal petition for citizenship. He was subsequently arrested and deported on the grounds of unlawful entry. Yet he had a good record of war service on a United States military transport.

Others had only a month or two, some only days, to go before they would become qualified to naturalize, but the 1950 McCarran Act quashed their hopes of becoming American citizens. Ironically, a few years ago maritime authorities were begging these alien seamen to stay on the ships, promising: "Remember, you can become a citizen if you complete five years."

Even before the first McCarran Act, this promise had a catch to it. For it takes about eight years to chalk up "an aggregate period of five years," as the law phrases it, because periods ashore in the United States, idled by a maritime strike or simply waiting to ship out again, do not count. However, for the landlubber alien the five years residence requirement means just that—five years.

Such a squawk went up from the thousands of alien crewmen who suddenly found in 1950 they had been, as many put it, robbed of their promised American citizenship that the privilege was restored—for one year—in the 1952 McCarran Act. A provision was inserted that unlawfully entered seamen who had acquired five years sea service before September 30, 1950, effective date of the Internal Security Act, could become citizens, if they filed a petition within a year—that is, before December 24, 1953. However, a joker was also inserted. These seamen were made subject to another provision which bars naturalization if a warrant of arrest or warrant of deportation is outstanding. So, if a seaman applies for the citizenship once more promised in this act, an immigration official can serve him with a warrant of arrest on the ground he is unlawfully in the country.

There are various ways the immigration official can stymie a seaman's try for citizenship. He can simply issue him what is called a D-1 card, which bars his discharge at an American port. That makes him a prisoner aboard his ship while his ship is in port. And if he cannot come ashore, he cannot go into court to petition for naturalization. Even if he is permitted to come ashore, the limit at any one time is twenty-nine days. If he tries to naturalize, he will have to overstay his time limit, because the law says that, with several exceptions, no final hearing shall be held within thirty days after the filing of a petition. (It usually takes from six to seven weeks.) So, if he overstays his time limit trying to become a citizen, he will be subject to deportation.

In fact, he need not overstay the twenty-nine-day limit to find himself in a jam. He is subject to arrest and deportation if at any time during the twenty-nine days he offers evidence orally, by writing, or by his conduct that he plans to remain in the United States longer than the twenty-nine days. He might remark innocently enough, "I'm going to become a citizen and settle down in this great country." No, he won't become a citizen and settle down—not if an informer were within earshot. A Peruvian crewman, coming ashore off an American vessel, was overheard to comment, "I want to find out how I can fix my papers so I can stay in the United States." He was deported as being what Immigration calls a *mala fide* seaman. Deported for that innocuous remark, he can never come back.

Sometimes the treatment accorded alien seamen—even those serving on vessels operated by or for the United States government—bears a resemblance to the persecution attributed ordinarily to the Iron Curtain countries. Take the case of Alexander Lobanov.

Lobanov's troubles stem from the day he joined the Boy Scouts in his native Leningrad. Soon afterward the Boy Scouts became by edict of the Soviets the Young Pioneers, the Red indoctrination outfit for the kiddies. At the age of fourteen he was automatically graduated into the Komsomols, or Young Communist League. He never took an active role in the Komsomols, but retained his card for economic reasons: it meant job preference.

He went to sea in 1928. Russian seamen must sign a

paper promising they will not go anywhere ashore alone or read foreign papers, answer questions about Russia, or visit any homes in foreign ports. He ignored the rule and after he saw what was going on in the outside world he quit the Komsomols. At a Soviet function in Portland, Oregon, in 1943, he spoke his mind about freedom in the United States. A Soviet naval officer present struck him, and Lobanov returned the blow. For all this he was ordered back to Russia. He refused to go. One night two Soviet agents waylaid him, slugged and kidnapped him, but he escaped into police protection by raising a rumpus at a traffic stop.

In 1945 Lobanov was permitted to ship as a seaman on American vessels. At every American port he was held aboard under guard and grilled by immigration inspectors, because he had no travel documents. Finally, in 1947, the State Department granted him a continuous waiver of passport. Even so, in January, 1951, a few months after the Internal Security Act went into effect, he was hauled off a Navy tanker in San Francisco and locked up.

For seven months the bewildered Lobanov paced the barracks-like room in detention quarters. Then the San Francisco *News* broke the story. Goaded by the press, the immigration authorities hastily convened a Board of Special Inquiry.

"If you were to return to the Soviet Union, would your life or liberty be in jeopardy?" Lobanov was asked.

"They would beat a confession out of me," he replied, "and put me on trial as an American spy, then put me in a concentration camp or kill me."

"Why didn't you break with the Communists sooner?"

"It takes a lot of hesitation," said Lobanov. "On a Soviet ship how many guys do you think would like to jump ship? About 75 per cent, but they are afraid."

Despite preponderant evidence of his loyalty to American ideals, the board ordered Lobanov excluded—to be sent back to Russia—because, as a youth some twenty-three years earlier, he had belonged to the Komsomols. This information did not come from any independent investigation, but from Lobanov himself.

Typical of Immigration tactics in this case was the stratagem now attempted by Bruce Barber, district director of immigration at San Francisco. He offered to allow Lobanov to sail on the guano boats plying between Galapagos and the West Coast. But Lobanov's counsel, Ernest Besig, San Francisco director of the American Civil Liberties Union, scotched that ruse. As pointed out by Art Caylor, columnist on the San Francisco *News,* Lobanov, without travel documents of any kind, would indeed have been a man without a country, forever sailing the guano boats, never permitted to step ashore.

Besig appealed. Nearly fourteen months after Lobanov had been picked off the Navy tanker, the Board of Immigration Appeals ruled that he had "met the burden of proving by convincing evidence that his affiliation with a proscribed organization was involuntary."

A friend said of Lobanov at the time: "He will kiss the stones in the street, he is so happy to be in this country."

Lobanov's elation was premature. He is not yet in this country, and it is problematical that he ever will be. He had been accumulating sea time with the dream of becoming an American citizen, but the Internal Security Act of 1950 suddenly dashed all hope. He does not qualify for the limited generosity offered to seamen in his category by the 1952 McCarran Act, even though he had served honorably on American ships, some of them Navy tankers, since 1945. The West Coast maritime strikes of 1946 and 1948, during which he was "beached" in the United States, prevented him from attaining the "aggregate period of five years" of sea service required for naturalization. Despite the fact that he has now piled up nearly six years of honorable sea service on American vessels; despite the fact that Immigration back in 1943 aided his efforts to keep out of Soviet clutches; despite the fact that the Appeal Board ruled his loyalty was not suspect, he cannot naturalize in any case because Immigration has consistently refused to grant him lawful entry.

Instead, Immigration continues to make it tougher for Lobanov. After his release from detention, Lobanov went back to sea on another Navy tanker. When his ship docked at San Francisco last April an immigration inspector assigned him a D-1 card, which prevented his going ashore. However, he was taken finally before District Director Barber who, Lobanov says, "ran me through a mental third degree in the most refined fashion."

Barber, he says, suggested putting him on a ship of Greek, Panamanian, or some other foreign registry. "I told Mr. Barber," says Lobanov, "that it would be extremely dangerous because those ships do go to the Iron Curtain countries. To this Mr. Barber asked me—why did

I think it would be dangerous for me to venture behind the Iron Curtain? That is how he puts a thorn in your brain. I asked him why I have been treated for eight years not as a political refugee but as a runaway seaman. To this Mr. Barber said nothing, he only gave me one of his most charming smiles."

Lobanov's only hope lies in gaining entry into the United States as a Russian quota immigrant—a slim hope in itself because Russia, with an annual quota of 2,798, has a waiting list of 46,292 visa applicants outside the Iron Curtain, and Russian DP's have "mortgaged" the quota to the year 1980.

Even so, to apply for such a visa, Lobanov will have to get into some other country. This offers a major obstacle, because he has no passport. But say another country does grant him temporary entrance. He will then run into the American consular curtain. In view of his one-time membership in the Komsomols, and the suspicion aroused by his Jean Valjean troubles with the Immigration Service, it seems highly improbable that any consular officer will run the risk of exposure to possible congressional censure by granting him a visa. It is so much simpler, and safer, to deny a visa.

And so Lobanov appears doomed to remain a sort of human seaweed, forever floating, never able to sink roots in any land.

Chapter

14   In the panic that sees a Red behind every visa, the McCarran Act ironically offers—next to Communism itself—one of the most serious threats to the welfare and security of the United States. Perhaps even the greatest, because the very fear that pervades Public Law 414, and is distilled by it, can be paralyzing.

This threat arises not only because the act denies civil liberties and impairs our relations with the rest of the democratic world in the lineup against totalitarianism. Few realize that possibly the gravest damage—some say irreparable—the act does is to our scientific program, which is at once the foundation of our national defense, of our expanding economy, and of our strength to invigorate backward nations in the global struggle against Communism. The McCarran Act smothers the free exchange of ideas with the rest of the free world's scientific community, particularly in the vital field of basic research. And thus it imperils the very life of the nation.

The Council of the American Physical Society, a nonpolitical organization representing virtually every physicist in the country, felt impelled to issue this warning at its

November, 1952, meeting in St. Louis: "In the past few years the progress of American physics has been impeded by United States visa and passport restrictions . . . Had similar regulations been in force prior to 1942, it is questionable if the United States would have developed the atomic bomb or have made great advances in radar."

Distinguished foreign scientists, even those outspokenly anti-Communist, are barred, for no expressed reason, from coming to the United States to share their knowledge, or their visas are stalled past the date of their usefulness. Roughly 50 per cent of the foreign scientists—among French scientists, from 70 to 80 per cent—are affected.

Various factors account for this. There is the hostility on the part of the law's administrators toward all foreigners. There is especially the deep, and rather strange, suspicion of all scientists. There is the consular underling's dread, almost abject, that he may incur the wrath of the so-called lunatic fringe in Congress if he passes a scientist whose remotest link to a cultural group now considered pinkish may be dredged up out of the dim past by some roving team of congressional investigators.

And the consular underling plays it safe: deny, or stall. He can err only in *granting* a visa.

This fear of foreign scientists—an instantaneous terror if the scientist has a reputation as a nuclear physicist—contradicts experience. We owe to foreign research the basic developments in radar and atomic energy. Penicillin, precursor of the "miracle drugs," was a foreign discovery. And since the war some of the most important contributions of science, such as the solving of the mystery of mesons, have been the products of foreign genius.

America's amazing technological feats—the cyclotrons, the bevatrons, the linear accelerators, the colossal plants that produce atomic energy—have given rise to the false impression that we have a world monopoly on brains. The McCarran Act tends to crystallize this fallacy that American know-how means American know-all. It just isn't so. Certainly we astound the world with our know-how, but we need blueprints before we can build. The carpenter and the bricklayer are not the architects of the magnificent structure they skillfully erect. And most of the blueprints for our incredible machines came from fundamental research done in foreign countries.

In the world of the scientist there is no such thing as a secret. True scientists do not hide their theories until they can get out a copyright or patent; they share their discoveries and, by sharing, learn. This, of course, is not to be confused with the top secrecy accorded atomic-bomb developments—a secrecy rightly required for security reasons. But let us keep in mind that it was the theoretical researchers—notably the immigrant Albert Einstein—who blazed the nuclear trail. German scientists in 1938 produced the first fission in uranium, and British science did the spade work in the production of plutonium.

Scientists share their discoveries through articles in the journals of their societies, supplemented by papers delivered at international conferences. These conferences are extremely important because techniques—of gamma-ray spectroscopy, for instance, or miraculous chest surgery—

can best be described in first-hand reports. Here is where we suffer the greatest blows to our welfare and prestige, because the harsh visa policy established by the 1952 McCarran Act and its predecessor, the 1950 McCarran Act, discourage the attendance of foreign scientists at conferences in America. As a result, in the past year the United States has lost five important conferences—the scheduled conferences of the International Congress of Psychology, the International Congress of Genetics, the International Astronomical Union, the International Federation of Documentation, and the International Physiological Congress. They were transferred to Canada and other countries. And no future conferences of any international group are being scheduled for the United States.

Commented the *Manchester Guardian,* the renowned British newspaper: "This visa business is doing the United States incalculable harm and is undoing all the lavish propaganda about its noble leadership of the free world . . . Most countries have their immigration absurdities, but there are aspects of the McCarran Act that go beyond mere bureaucratic arbitrariness and are repugnant to civilized intercourse."

Samuel A. Goudsmit, senior scientist at Brookhaven National Laboratory, scene of atomic research, says: "The numerous traveling fellowships available to scientists in the 'twenties have, in proportion, contributed much more to solving the problems of atomic structure than the amounts spent on building laboratories. Every international scientific meeting marks a step forward in the development of science . . . We cannot afford to be cut off from this vital source of human progress."

Howard A. Meyerhoff, representing the American Association for the Advancement of Science, advised the President's Commission: "If this trend continues, American science faces the threat not merely of becoming provincial but also of becoming atrophied to the point where the national welfare and national security will suffer. Security and welfare are founded on knowledge, only part of which originates within the confines of the United States."

The Atomic Energy Commission pointed out: "Nuclear physics and chemistry, for example, are fields where more basic knowledge is urgently needed and where the traditionally free exchange of basic scientific information is essential to maximum progress. Foreign science can and does make really significant contributions to these fields."

In his retiring presidential address at the Cambridge, Massachusetts, meeting of the American Physical Society on January 23, 1953, Professor J. H. Van Vleck of Harvard said: "We have spent billions on the Marshall Plan, and then alienate much of the resulting good will by an unsympathetically and woodenly administered visa policy. This situation reminds one of the railroad that lavishes a mint of money on new streamliners and then lets the conductor insult the passengers . . .

"On one point I want to be clear—our classified information must be zealously guarded. There is danger that we be diverted from this if we dissipate our efforts at security on the trivial rather than on the important. For example, we fingerprint both the tourist and the classified worker. The moment we start guarding our toothbrushes and diamond rings with equal zeal, we usually lose fewer toothbrushes but more diamond rings."

Every good American agrees with the idea of excluding active Communists or agents of the Kremlin who would come here to advance the cause of Communism in the United States. But most of the barred scientists are outright anti-Communists—men who in the idealism of youth may have embraced some pinkish cause as an antidote for the poverty of the early 'thirties or as a counter-irritant to rising Nazism, became bitterly disillusioned, and are now hostile to Communism. These scientists, far removed from the political attachments of their youth, are being penalized, not by their own governments, but by the United States.

As if such punishment were not absurd enough, there is actually no security consideration involved. The conferences from which these eminent men are excluded are open scientific meetings on non-classified, unrestricted subjects. And the professors invited to teach, lecture or do research at our universities would have no more access to secret information than the man on the street.

Consular ineptitude and fear of congressional censure are not alone to blame. The McCarran Act aggravated the predicament of the visiting professor by changing his status to that of a "skilled alien." Formerly, he came as a non-quota immigrant. Now, if coming to fill a permanent position in a university, he must fall in at the end of the quota line, in some countries an almost interminable queue. If he has been invited to attend a conference, he will need a visitor's visa, and for that he must undergo the same rigid consular screening as an alien applying for permanent residence. And he must satisfy all the health, financial, security and other requirements of the permanent immigrant even if he seeks only a transit visa to stop off in New York for a few hours en route to a conference in Canada or South America.

And so, if the McCarran Act had been in effect before the last war, a man like physicist Enrico Fermi, classified as a "skilled alien" and subject to heightened consular trepidation because of his reputation as a nuclear scientist, might still be waiting in quota-starved Italy for a visa. Our own atomic scientists agree that without the help of this famed Italian immigrant, who built the first atomic pile in 1942, we may not have developed the A-bomb in time to end the last World War as abruptly as we did.

A singular case of consular incompetence harassed Professor Michael Polanyi, eminent British chemist and social philosopher, long recognized as Britain's foremost anti-Communist scholar. He has never nurtured any left-wing leanings; rather, since 1917, he has been an active crusader against the strictures of Communism, and one of the earliest writers to expose the Soviet propaganda myths. In recognition of his staunch battling for intellectual freedom, he was awarded an honorary doctorate by Princeton University in 1946.

Professor Polanyi was elected to a Chair of Social Philosophy at the University of Chicago, his appointment to begin October 1, 1951. He applied to the American consul at Liverpool for a permanent visa on January 20th of that

Soviet system. This, after nine months investigation of my political views and activities!

"I found it revolting that they questioned me on the political opinions of my brother, who is a professor at Columbia University, New York. I answered that he had no doubt sincerely expressed his views in his writings—which placed the matter beyond the ken of my questioners."

In June, 1952, eighteen months after he had applied for the visa, the consulate announced he was "inadmissible into the United States" because of "certain political beliefs or activities; and . . . membership in, or affiliation with, certain organizations."

Professor Polanyi was flabbergasted.

"Americans," he points out, "are free to enter the countries of Western Europe without even being required to have a visa. They are heartily welcome here. But it is a shame that Europeans who would visit America in return should have to undergo a political investigation extending over many months by officials without any knowledge of European affairs and should be eventually rejected by such persons with a blast of libelous accusations against their political honesty. This is bound to poison the friendship between Americans and Europeans.

"The remedy lies in a simple act of imagination. Let any American go carefully through the whole list of conditions imposed upon West European visitors to the United States and imagine himself to be subjected to the same conditions when he travels to Europe—while at the same time West Europeans could enter the United States without let or hindrance. He would be horrified to realize that such a position exists today in reverse."

The hardships entailed naturally intensify the resentments. The scientist invited to an American university for an academic year arranges for the care of his laboratory during his absence, resigns his European post, sublets his house, books passage—and, when it's too late to make new plans, the visa is rejected. Furthermore, our visa policy embarrasses our Western friends in their own fight against their Communist countrymen. In fact, those who *are* granted visas are sometimes suspected of being American agents.

Edward A. Shils, professor of social sciences at the University of Chicago, who guest-edited a special issue (October, 1952) of the *Bulletin of the Atomic Scientists* on this subject, asked for contributions by European scientists on their visa troubles. He reported: "Some to whom we wrote, including several who had been most unjustly treated, were reluctant to contribute because they feared that in the present state of European opinion, the truth about their experiences under the McCarran Act was so discreditable to the United States that it would aid the Communists and other enemies of the United States."

Professor Shils added that European scientists, though their faith in America has been profoundly shaken, nevertheless retain that faith because "of their close friendships with American scientists and scholars and, in some cases, their deeper political convictions that, in the long run, the moral substance and good sense of America will reassert itself and we will discard this rough-handed and frivolous policy."

In an address before a scientific gathering in Washington on August 8, 1952, Assistant Secretary of State John D. Hickerson declared: "With a feeling of humility, I say: We Americans recognize how directly our own progress and well-being are related to the scientific achievements of other nations, and we are ever ready to give others the understanding and the respect which we ourselves seek to merit."

So?

E. A. Pringsheim, professor of botany at the University of Cambridge and an outstanding authority on algae, was on the faculty of Charles University in Prague when the Nazis came to Czechoslovakia. He took refuge in England in 1939 and became a naturalized British citizen in 1947.

Professor Pringsheim was invited by Yale University to give a lecture course during the spring term of 1952 and to establish a center of algal research at Yale. He was also asked to start a collection of algal cultures both at Yale and at the Hopkins Marine Station in California. He also received urgent invitations to lecture at Vanderbilt University, Harvard, Indiana University, and the University of California. He was also scheduled to give the introductory address at a joint meeting of the New York Academy of Science and the Society of Protozoologists. He was also invited to read papers at meetings of the Bacteriological and the Phycological Societies of America.

Professor Pringsheim had a busy schedule lined up, and certainly America stood to gain immeasurably from his visit. The professor said he had "hoped to give as well as take by teaching my methods, and also by seeing a life's work crowned by the certainty that it would be continued in the United States."

He applied for a visa in good time. He produced the necessary documents, some of them difficult to obtain as a former refugee. He filled in various forms. He answered a lengthy questionnaire. He underwent several interviews. He was finally told that the visa would be forthcoming in a few days. Instead, he received a letter stating that his "entry is deemed to be prejudicial to the interests of the United States."

Professor Pringsheim was shocked. He says: "I have been a biologist during the whole of my adult life, that is, fifty years, mainly interested in science, art, and my family, and devoting to politics only the minimum of time I believed my duty. In Czechoslovakia I had kept away from politics altogether. In Britain, I had voted three times, twice Liberal, the last time Conservative. I am and always have been opposed to Communism. What the refusal meant I cannot guess, nor could the science attaché of the United States Embassy [in London] tell me the reason . . . I was grievously hurt by a decision which I cannot understand."

Twenty-four foreign physicists were invited to attend an International Congress on Nuclear Physics at the University of Chicago in 1951. The visas of eight physicists were held up, among them Professor Rudolph E. Peierls, head of the Mathematical Physics Department of the University of Birmingham and a Fellow of the Royal Society. He applied for his visa in March and got it late in November, two months *after* the conference had adjourned.

However, Professor Peierls *was* able to attend. It so happened that, while an American consular officer in England was pondering him as a security risk, the professor was in Washington on a British diplomatic passport participating in an official Anglo-American conference on the declassification of highly classified atomic energy information.

He went on to Chicago from Washington. By dallying over his visa application, the consular officer would have prevented the professor from attending the Chicago meeting had he not already been in the United States—yet the Chicago conference dealt with no classified material whatsoever.

The Office of Naval Research, certainly conscious of United States security, was co-sponsor of the Chicago congress. A high official let it be known that the naval office would sponsor no more international conferences so long as the present McCarran Act visa policy remained in effect.

Another scientist invited to the Chicago conference was Professor M. L. Oliphant, FRS, director of the Research School of Physical Science, Australian National University, formerly on the faculty at the University of Birmingham, England. His contributions to the development of radar were described in an official United States publication as "probably the most important single item of reverse lend-lease." In 1943 he came to America to arrange for British teams to join in the United States atomic energy project.

He too applied early for a visa to attend the Chicago

conference and, assured there would be no difficulty, booked airline passage, which he had to cancel. He never did get a visa. The American consulate in Sydney still insists that the visa "had not been refused, but that there were administrative delays." Professor Oliphant learned indirectly there was no question of Communist sympathies involved, but that the "administrative delays" were caused by his criticism of American policy in the field of atomic energy, indicating the State Department may believe in freedom of speech—but not for foreigners.

Public Law 414 gives a consul discretion to issue a visa to an ex-Red who has "actively opposed" Communism for five years. However, before the reformed Communist, or Communist sympathizer, can be admitted to the United States he must also establish his active change of heart "to the satisfaction of the attorney general." It doesn't stop there. The attorney general must then make a detailed report to Congress.

This procedure proved too repugnant to Jacques Monod, member of the famed Institut Pasteur in Paris. Invited here by the American Chemical Society and the Harvey Society, he was denied a visa on the grounds he had been a member of the Communist Party from 1943 to 1945. The American consul in Paris suggested he apply to the attorney general for special permission to enter the United States temporarily.

Professor Monod declined. He deplored the "extremely distasteful obligation of personally submitting my 'case' to the Department of Justice and of having to ask for permission to enter the United States as an exceptional and temporary favor of which I am legally assumed to be unworthy." He also looked upon swearing to a "biographical statement" as too remindful of "a sad and terrible experience: this kind of inquisition was introduced into the French Administration under the Nazi Occupation."

"This being said," the professor told the consul, "I should like to add that I did not reach this decision lightheartedly, as I fully realize that it means cutting myself partially away from a country which I love and to which I am attached by very strong links. Not only am I half-American, but I have many very close friends in your country."

Daniel Chalonge, a leading French astronomer, was invited to the University of Chicago as a research associate for three months, with use of the university's MacDonald Observatory in Texas during January, 1949. He states he was subjected to "an insolent and stupid interrogation" by the American consul in Paris. Finally, he was given to understand, *in March,* that his visa had already been approved—*in January.*

Professor Chalonge said that was all right, he would still take the visa. The consul replied in dismay: "But I thought you could not go after January." Professor Chalonge explained that the university had extended its invitation to the following year. And so, the visa approved in January, as announced in March, was cancelled in April.

Professor E. B. Chain, British Nobel Prize laureate, co-discoverer of penicillin, and member of the United Nations Health Commission, was refused a visa. Probable cause: several trips to Eastern European countries as an official of the U.N. Health Commission to promote penicillin production.

Charles Sadron, professor of physics at the University of Strasbourg, was designated an official French delegate to the 1951 chemistry congress in New York. "As I am a member of the Committee on Macromolecular Chemistry, I naturally had to attend," he declared. He didn't. He was not even given the honor of an official reply to his visa application. But he was given another honor—the scheduling of the next International Conference on Macromolecules at Strasbourg.

Bruno Ferretti, theoretical physicist of Rome's Marconi Institute of Physics, was invited to the Institute for Advanced Study at Princeton for the academic year 1951-52. Fourteen months after he requested a visa it was still not forthcoming. It cost him much hardship, including $100 to cancel steamship reservations.

"I sincerely confess," says Professor Ferretti, "that I cannot understand why it is so difficult for me to get an American visa. There are no special political reasons since I do not belong to any political party . . . [And] everyone sees that general questions on quantum electro-dynamics are hardly dangerous for the security of any country."

The tragedy, of course, is that the United States desperately needs theoretical scientists. As in any field, there are long gaps between theory, blueprint and ultimate production. Right now, because of the restrictive visa policy that bars too many great thinkers, physicists say we lag far behind in basic research. At stake is our national security. Despite that, the list of visa denials is almost endless. Nor is it confined to European scientists.

Mexican physicists boycotted the 1951 meeting of the American Physical Society because two delegates were denied visas. Neither was affiliated with any left-wing organization, and one of them, Dr. Marcos Moshinsky, held a State Department fellowship at Princeton for three years.

Dr. Leonardo Guzman, professor of medicine at the University of Santiago, former Prime Minister and Minister of Education of the Chilean Republic, was educated in the United States. Chile's most enthusiastic pro-American, he had made frequent trips to the United States on his diplomatic passport. As director of the Radium Institute of Santiago and a foremost cancer researcher, he had even visited the University of California's Radiation Laboratory, the Argonne Laboratory at Chicago and Oak Ridge.

In November, 1952, Dr. Guzman was pleased to get an invitation to a symposium at the Georgia Medical School in Augusta. This would afford him the opportunity, while in the United States, to learn more about isotopes for his cancer work. He sent his diplomatic passport to the United States Embassy in Santiago for a visa. An American consular officer summoned him, gave the former Prime Minister an interrogative working over, then refused him a visa.

Dr. Guzman was astounded.

He says: "I called his attention to my previous trips, my membership in many American scientific societies and academies, and especially to the fact that I am an Honorary Fellow of the College of Radiology of North America. I asked for an explanation of this attitude and his interference, which was unusual, on account of my having a diplomatic passport.

"Then I went to see the Ambassador and was deeply impressed by the anomalous position of this gentleman: he was under the actual supervision of his consul. This reminded me of the Nazi and Communist organizations: the ambassadors and apparent heads of diplomatic missions are submitted to the undignified superiority and close control of employees who should normally be under their command."

Instead of America, Dr. Guzman went to Europe where, he reported, everyone "talks about the arrogance and intolerance of the United States in trying to determine the future of humanity and to influence each man and each nation's actions."

Others too report a growing disaffection. Marcus Cunliffe, lecturer in American Studies at the University of Manchester, says our visa policy persuades Europeans that "America is in the grip of foolish and frightened men who can no longer distinguish friend from foe, let alone realize that even honest and intelligent men make mistakes."

Professor Raymond Aron, French political analyst and a chief protagonist of the North Atlantic-anti-Communist policy in French journalism, assails the assumption that the denial of visas is aimed solely—and "this would be the only reasonable aim"—at keeping out persons suspected of totalitarian sympathies and capable of endangering the security of the United States.

"The persons," he says, "who are most dangerous to the security of the United States certainly must have a faultless dossier in which there is never any trace of affiliation with a Communist party. Really dangerous Communists belong to underground networks, and they are probably inaccessible to the powers of the McCarran Act."

Our closed-door policy works both ways. It keeps alien scientists out; it keeps domestic scientists in. And thus, in a sense, it makes hypocrisy an official government policy. We strongly advocate free travel as a way to ease world tensions through a greater understanding among peoples. We censure Russia for not permitting Soviet citizens to go forth and see how the other half of the world lives. But if Russia did grant exit to her citizens, the McCarran Act would bar them from seeing how America lives, despite the fact that a taste of free enterprise is often a sure way of effecting a change of heart.

In the face of our advocacy of free travel among nations, what do *we* do?

Take the celebrated case of Linus Pauling, the California Institute of Technology scientist who was denied a passport to attend a discussion on the structure of proteins arranged by the Royal Society of London in May, 1952. No specific reason was given other than his trip abroad would not be "in the interests of the United States."

S. D. Boykin, director of the Office of Security and Consular Affairs, indicated Professor Pauling's "anti-Communist statements had been sufficiently strong," but it had been reported he had "made statements criticizing the United States." (No freedom of speech here either?) Boykin asked the professor to explain those statements.

"However," says the baffled professor, "he said that he was not at liberty to tell me what the reputed statements were."

Pauling admitted he had at times expressed political opinions contrary to the official opinions of the government—some of them similar to sentiments voiced by the late Senator Robert A. Taft. He produced a loyalty oath and evidence he had been under vicious attack by Russia. Still no good.

Pauling was later invited to a London meeting of the Faraday Society on the physical chemistry of proteins. Another refusal of a passport prompted Senator Wayne Morse to denounce in Congress this limitation of the freedom of travel by American citizens. Pauling was promised a passport if he would swear once again he was not and never had been a Communist. He took the second oath and got the passport. His case is by no means exceptional.

There is still another bizarre aspect to this problem. Under the McCarran Act we even keep foreigners from going home, once they get here. Scores of Chinese students fall in this category. They are given no hearings, are not told why they can't go home. One young Chinese who came to the University of California on a student visa now finds the continental United States his prison, despite the fact that his professors testified he had learned nothing of any security value.

Still, the greatest threat to our national welfare lies in the power the McCarran Act places in the hands of consular underlings, who exhibit such an ineptitude for so much authority. Their shortcomings were neatly capsuled in the experience of Professor R. G. W. Norrish of the University of Cambridge, invited to Stanford University some months ago. The consular officer who interviewed him on his application for a visa asked what he had ever written, if anything. Among other works Professor Norrish modestly listed a volume entitled *Free Radicals*.

Professor Norrish was nonplussed at the vice consul's sudden look of shock and horror. When the questioning instantly swung to left-wingers, it dawned on the professor. He had quite a time convincing the consular officer there was nothing subversive about his book—even after he explained it dealt only with "transient intermediaries in chemical reactions."

Chapter

15 Not the least among the criticisms of the McCarran Act is that it substitutes for the American criterion of individual worth and dignity a standard that measures people on the basis of where they come from and whether they were paragons there.

Yes, paragons. For how else would you describe the quota immigrants who must possess "the high education, technical training, specialized experience, or exceptional ability" that would be "substantially beneficial prospectively to the national economy, cultural interests, or welfare of the United States"? The McCarran Act, apparently in awe of this mythical immigrant it creates, makes no attempt to elucidate. It passes that chore along to the attorney general, who must determine whether the immigrant falls within such a category of approved human beings.

This category is called the First Preference Quota. The law sets aside 50 per cent of each quota for these exemplary creatures. Even so, none can attempt to qualify unless there is a specific request by an American employer to the attorney general for help of this unusual sort.

Congressman Walter, co-author of Public Law 414, styles this preferential treatment "a policy of selectivity." Others, more realistic, define it as a policy of "rejectivity."

Alice W. O'Connor, secretary of the Massachusetts Displaced Persons Commission, told the President's Commission at its Boston hearing: "Nothing in the experience of those who were concerned with the Displaced Persons program warrants optimism about the desire for placement in America of persons of high learning, and so forth . . .

"Many learned professions—the law, medicine, pharmacy—have tightened their regulations for licensing. States [not all] have established citizenship as a condition precedent to licensing. Moreover, there appears to be, neither within the Immigration Service nor in the consular service, any body of men trained to know occupational skills or qualified to evaluate who is of high education, specialized experience, and so forth. There is also needed a definition as to what is meant by 'specialized experience' and 'exceptional ability.' Sheepherders, for example, of Basque national origin, are apparently not within this group . . .

"Public Law 414 uses the device of occupational skills as a secondary method to restrict immigration."

Many great Americans who founded fabulous industries in this country—among them Andrew Carnegie, the steel tycoon who was a Scottish immigrant, and Henry C. Frick, the Swiss immigrant of coal-and-iron fame—would have been barred under Public Law 414. They came as unskilled laborers.

The way Mr. Walter puts it, this new system of selectivity sounds quite simple and wonderful: "If, for example, diemakers are in short supply, companies needing such skilled labor appeal to the Department of Justice, which, through the U. S. Employment Service, verifies the need and instructs our overseas representatives to give preferred status to such workers."

Let's see how simple and wonderful it is. Say, for example, you have a friend in Luxemburg, a skilled machinist, who has been begging you to help him emigrate to America with his family. Your Uncle Harry owns a machine shop. He says, "Sure, I'll sponsor your friend. Matter of fact, I could use a good machinist."

This is the Nut-house-that-Jack-built routine he must pursue:

First, he goes to the Immigration Service, which must determine whether the immigrant is entering as a skilled alien for permanent residence, or on a temporary basis for temporary services. That settled, Uncle Harry is referred to the employment people to get three certified copies of a clearance order.

He places an order for clearance with the local office of the State Employment Service. There are certain standards to be met: the wage he offers to pay the immigrant must be the prevailing wage; the qualifications Uncle Harry lists for the worker must conform to State and Federal rules; the job itself must not be unreasonable, such as hand-rubbing fuzz off peaches.

The local office, satisfied that Uncle Harry's order meets all these requirements, checks employment sources locally to see if there is a qualified machinist available. If it can't find such a man, the order is referred to:

The Area Clearance Office, which distributes the order to local offices throughout its area. And if none of these offices can find such a man, the matter is referred to:

The State Clearance Office, which clears the order on a statewide basis. If no such man can be found in the state, then neighboring states are queried. And if they can't supply a man, then the order is referred to:

The regional office of the United States Employment Service, which checks the other states within its region. And if they can't find a man, then the order is referred to:

The Bureau of Employment Security in Washington, which may request additional information. In that event, the order goes back to the beginning and starts all over again.

But if the Bureau of Employment Security has no question, it checks the rest of the nation. And if that fails to produce a man for this job, then Uncle Harry receives a little slip of paper that says: "We are unable to find a qualified domestic worker."

By now, Uncle Harry's head is spinning faster than the wheels in his shop. But he's a stubborn fellow. He's going to see this through if it's the last thing he does—and, like many another United States employer, it *is* the last thing of this sort he ever does.

Uncle Harry takes the clearance slip, in triplicate, to the immigration bureau. An official there may reject it, for reasons of his own.

But let's say he okays it. It then goes to the attorney general, who may turn it down.

But let's say he okays it. It then goes to the State Department, where some official may reject it.

But let's say he okays it. It then goes to the American consulate nearest the Luxemburg machinist.

And there some underling, also for reasons of his own, can deny the machinist a visa. And that ends that.

Perhaps an eminent Italian radiologist, on a visit to Denver, falls in love with the city, its people and climate, and decides to settle there. Very simple to stay under a First Preference Quota? No, indeed. He must have a hospital petition for his services—and run this red-tape gauntlet.

At intervals the attorney general issues a list showing a national shortage existing in certain callings. A recent list included chemists, college presidents and deans, dentists, physicians and surgeons, teachers, trained nurses, metallurgists, tool and die designers.

Employers or institutions needing such help can skip the employment service rigmarole and apply directly to the Immigration Service and go on from there. But there's still that consular officer at the end of the line. And there's still such a thing as a license to practice under state laws, if the immigrant gets here.

Certain "skilled aliens" do not require a clearance from Immigration as a normal practice. These include authors, sculptors, dramatic readers, marimba bandsmen, masters of ceremony, ring-masters, missionaries, and, cheeringly, comedians.

That is how the First Preference Quota operates. The sub-subsection in the law dealing with this preference is only one paragraph, 119 words. Yet a regional official of the U. S. Employment Service, a gentleman of serious mien, told me: "We had a meeting of regional directors in Washington and spent a half day going over this provision, with an expert explaining it to us. Later, we held a half-day meeting for state employment directors, explaining it to them. You know"—and he gave me a quizzical look— "I'll be darned if I understand it yet."

An unsavory aspect of this new provision is that it opens a fertile field for graft that would be extremely hard to detect. An unscrupulous employer could sponsor an immigrant for a stiff fee. And the immigrant, paying the price, would certainly not feel inclined to expose the practice and thereby make himself deportable once he gets here.

Partly because of our restricted immigration, there has long been a shortage in agricultural workers. This is partially solved throughout the West by the importation of contract Mexican laborers—and, illegally, by the so-called "wetbacks," the Mexicans who sneak across the border to work the crops and, because of their illegal status, are often exploited. Here is another paradox. We round up these wetbacks at great expense—often in raids without a search warrant—and transport them back across the border under guard. Then we bring them in again by the thousands, under contract. Once the crops are gathered, out they go too.

One California rancher discovered four exceptional workers among a batch of "lawful" Mexican laborers.

They were so skilled he wanted to keep them on, was even willing to give them individual five-year contracts at top wages. But that was impossible. Mexico, like all other countries in the Western Hemisphere, is a nonquota nation. The citizens of these countries need no quota number to come here, providing they meet other qualifications under the immigration law. However, the First Preference Quota does not apply to Mexico and the other non-quota countries in this part of the world. And so, the California rancher could not keep these skilled aliens, already working on his place, once their contracts under the special United States-Mexico agreement had expired.

That brings up another inconsistency in Public Law 414. Under Section 203 (a) (1), skilled aliens are admissible if they have an employer to sponsor them—the First Preference Quota clause. Under Section 212 (a) (14), aliens seeking to enter the United States for the purpose of performing either skilled or unskilled labor are barred.

There are other preferences besides the first. A second preference sets aside the next 30 per cent of each quota to qualified aliens who are the parents of American citizens —if their children are at least twenty-one years of age. At first glance this sounds wonderful too, but actually it can penalize a man for not marrying early in life and starting a family at once.

A good example is the case of Dominic Casini, an alien Italian. He walked off an Italian ship in Philadelphia in November of 1924 with other crew members to see the sights of the city. He liked what he saw and decided to stay.

In the nearly thirty years since, he has never been involved in any crime, nor has he ever attempted to conceal the manner of his entry.

Casini married an American girl in the early 'thirties, and two sons were born, one now nineteen, the other fifteen years of age. The Casinis separated several years ago.

He applied for citizenship in 1939, but was turned down because there was no record of his entry. He frankly told the immigration officials at that time that he had jumped ship at Philadelphia in 1924. No action was taken against him, and to Casini that was further reassurance that his presence was not, as Immigration is fond of saying, "prejudicial to the interests of the United States." He went about his business.

When the Alien Registration Act was passed in 1940, Casini readily complied. They questioned him, gave him a card, and took no action. Further reassurance.

In obedience to the McCarran Act, Casini applied at the Immigration Service for a new alien "ID" card. They "discovered" there was no record of his entry twenty-nine years ago, immediately issued a warrant for his arrest. The hearing officer gave him the choice of voluntary departure or deportation.

If deported, he could never come back. Even so, voluntary departure meant he had to return to Italy and try to make it back under the quota—and there's a long, long waiting list in Italy. It may take him years just to get an appointment with an American consular officer, and then the official may not like the cut of Casini's jib and deny him a visa. If Casini's older son had been born two years sooner, Casini would have qualified for a preferential quota, and could have made it back in six months or less.

He could not get a suspension of the deportation order because, despite the fact that he contributed to the support of his sons, Immigration held that deporting him would not cause "exceptional and extremely unusual hardship" to his family, or him.

The irony of Casini's case—and many others in a similar fix—is that this age-limit catch to the Second Preference Quota gives Casini, a man of excellent moral character, less consideration than criminals long ago ordered deported but not deportable because no country will accept them.

To top off this irony with a bitter frosting, if Casini had walked off that ship in Philadelphia less than five months earlier—before July 1, 1924—he could have established a record of permanent admission by a simple registry process. Such a provision had been in the immigration statutes since 1929.

There is a Third Preference—the remaining 20 per cent of each quota going to qualified quota immigrants who are the spouses or children of aliens lawfully admitted for permanent residence. Here again instances of hardship, not defined as "exceptional or extremely unusual," occur. One woman, married to a lawfully admitted alien and mother of a United States citizen child, was ordered deported for illegal entry, with the alternative of voluntary departure. She went to Mexico and had to wait five months for a third preferential visa to get back.

Quota numbers of a quota area not used in the First Preference go into the Second Preference hamper, and any unused here go to the Third Preference. If any still remain, up to 25 per cent of the remainder go to brothers and sisters of American citizens, and to the children of American citizens who do not qualify for nonquota status.

Anything left over from all these preferences fall as crumbs to qualified non-preference quota immigrants. And that's another reason for the long queues in front of American consulates in many countries.

George Mardikian, the San Francisco chef, tells of a meeting he had a few years ago in Rome with Cardinal Agagianian, scholarly patriarch of Catholic Armenians. The conversation turned to America's immigration policies, and a gentle smile crept over the Cardinal's face.

"You know, Mr. Mardikian," he said, "I believe it is more difficult to get into your United States than to enter Heaven."

"Why do you say that, Your Eminence?"

"I don't think it can be so difficult for people to enter Heaven, because all they have to do is become good, clean citizens and do the right thing, and of course we in the church help them with our prayers." The Cardinal's smile spread. "Even for a saint, it's difficult to enter the United States."

Chapter

16   In Hong Kong today an estimated 6,000
children wait anxiously for the right to come to the United
States as derivative citizens. Many have been waiting for
years. Immigration lawyers familiar with the situation say
that, as a conservative guess, no more than 900 of these
children will ever make it. The others will lose their
American citizenship because they won't be able to get
here before their sixteenth birthday.

A lot will depend, however, on the interpretation the
American consulate at Hong Kong places on a new time
limit fixed by Public Law 414. The old law said a person
born overseas after May 26, 1934, one of whose parents was
an alien, could retain the United States citizenship of
the other parent if he reached the United States before
his sixteenth birthday.

Public Law 414 advanced the deadline of arrival to the
twenty-third birthday and said this new date applies to
those born after May 26, 1934. But whether it applies to
those who made application for travel documents before
the new law went into effect may be, in the view of the consulate, a different matter. It is significant that since the

effective date of Public Law 414 scarcely a handful of these youngsters have been permitted to come to the United States to press their claims of derivative citizenship.

Immigration lawyers assail this legislative edict, which puts a time limit on a person's arrival here, as unconstitutional because it places a condition on citizenship already held. And it is a condition that may be an unwarranted hardship.

For example, in the spring of 1952 a boy left Hong Kong by plane in time to reach Hawaii just before his sixteenth birthday. The plane was delayed a half day in Tokyo by mechanical trouble, and then slowed by stiff headwinds. The boy arrived in Honolulu on his sixteenth birthday. And so, by that fateful circumstance, he lost his derivative citizenship. Although the day previous he had been an American citizen he was refused entry as an alien without an immigrant visa.

He was held in detention for some weeks, finally paroled into the United States and allowed to apply for a suspension of the deportation order on the ground of economic detriment to his citizen father. (He couldn't have qualified for a stay of deportation under the new law.) His father eventually petitioned to have his ex-citizen son naturalized.

This boy's case—stalled for years by the ponderous machinery set up by the American consulate in Hong Kong —foretells the fate of the vast majority of the 6,000 derivative-citizen children still over there.

Prior to the Second World War a Chinese claiming derivative citizenship simply booked passage to the United

States, and upon his arrival the Immigration Service determined the validity of his claim. In the event of a denial, he had the right to seek judicial redress.

In 1941 President Roosevelt issued a proclamation forbidding citizens to leave or enter the United States without a passport or waiver of passport issued by the State Department. It was a wartime measure to prevent the entry of spies and saboteurs under the guise of American citizenship.

This proclamation remains in effect, and the Foreign Service relies upon it to justify a procedure that effectively blocks the efforts of the sons and daughters of American citizens to come here. No subversive angle is involved, for no checks whatever are made to determine whether the entry of these youngsters would be prejudicial to the interests of the United States from an internal security standpoint.

World War II cut off transportation from China and thus built up the backlog of 6,000 cases still pending. After the war, for the first time now that the passport rule was in effect, these Chinese-American citizens discovered they had to obtain consular approval before a steamship line would grant them passage.

Shortly after the war, it took about six months to process a consular approval. But gradually the procedure was refined until, by 1949, according to a State Department official's own statement in a court action, the processing period ran to four years and eight months. Estimates today put it at upwards of ten years—and by then most of the applicants are too old to get here. As one observer points out, it has become far easier for a nonquota alien Chinese to obtain an immigrant visa than for an American citizen of Chinese descent to get a travel document he is entitled to. Worse, unscrupulous "brokers" in Hong Kong milk the American fathers of large sums of money in spurious efforts to speed up action on their children's applications for such documents.

Under Public Law 414, consular officers now have the power to determine the validity of a claim of United States citizenship by a person abroad. In most cases the consular officer has no legal training. But that seems a small matter because he has the right to determine citizenship claims without a trial, without a hearing of any kind, without right to legal aid, without right to cross-examination of witnesses, without following rules of evidence, including hearsay, without making any written record on which the decision is based.

However, inasmuch as the thousands of young citizens stuck in Hong Kong had applied *before* the effective date of Public Law 414—and thus had applied for travel permits, not passports—their cases are being processed under the old setup.

A year or more may elapse before the applicant is summoned to the consulate and questioned on the basis of information received from the Immigration Service.

At any hour of the day or night, raids may be made on the child's home, where documents and papers helpful to him may be confiscated. These raids are made by the Hong Kong police, who are always accompanied by an observer from the American consulate. To protests from lawyers, the

Passport Office has replied: "It would seem appropriate for the Government of the United States to take such means as may be legally available to it in Hong Kong to protect itself against fraud." Or to protect itself against children of Chinese-Americans? In many instances, lawyers charge, the raids are conducted without warrants. Furthermore, they charge, the consulate requires the child applicant to go before a Hong Kong notary to make a statutory declaration, which renders him liable under the criminal laws of Hong Kong. If he is suspected of lying, the local authorities are informed, and the Chinese police of Hong Kong make an arrest and put the applicant under the third degree. Thus the United States Government joins in a scheme for the third degree, which is unlawful under our own laws.

In addition to all the procedural red tape the citizen child must undergo the indignity of radiological examinations—"bone tests" to determine if, perchance, he might be older than he says—and blood tests, to determine if he has the blood type of his parents.

Even worse, the blood-letting does not clinch a child's claim of citizenship. Mrs. R. B. Shipley, director of the Passport Office, informed Harold D. Kline, an immigration lawyer of San Francisco: "It happens occasionally that, although the blood groupings may prove to be compatible, the Department is satisfied from other evidence and information that the case is fraudulent. It is better . . . that the 'hundred' guilty be stopped at Hong Kong than that they be permitted to proceed to a port of the United States where, through legal maneuvering . . . they may gain admission to this country." (She was referring to the famous jurist's comment: "Better that 99 guilty go free than one innocent suffer.") Her distrust of the courts was evident: "It is certain that many persons who, in reality, were not citizens of the United States obtained declaratory judgments holding them to be citizens."

Now then, after all the years of consular red tape in Hong Kong, and the indignity of blood and bone tests, the citizen child at last sails for his father's homeland—if, of course, he has not by now passed the age limit.

Will he make it? Does all the cumbersome rigmarole entitle him to entry at an American port? Not at all. The travel document he acquired after such a costly falderal means nothing more than an okay to buy a ticket to travel to the United States. It doesn't entitle him to anything more. It simply relieves the steamship line of any criminal liability in the event the child is denied entry when he arrives.

Once the child reaches an American port, the Immigration Service takes over, as if nothing at all had happened. In the Hong Kong processing, no pretense is made by the consulate to determine the child's claim of citizenship under this old procedure. After all, the chief source of material and evidence, normally the father, is in the United States. (This still holds true, although the McCarran Act empowers consular officers to determine citizenship claims abroad.) So far as the child's right to enter the United States as a citizen is concerned, in these cases still being processed, the responsibility rests with the Immigration Service, where it had rested for more than fifty years.

Upon the child's arrival, he and his father are questioned, separately, to check their stories. No significance whatever is attached to the affidavit executed at the consulate in Hong Kong, nor the results of the lengthy procedural ordeal the child underwent. No value is accorded the prior questioning of the father by the immigration authorities, because the father presumably had the opportunity to apprise his son of the testimony he had given here. No account is taken of the child's interviews with the consulate, because Immigration has no record of such interviews.

The arriving child, within three days ordinarily, is either found to be a citizen and admitted or, if his claim is rejected, is ordered back to China. He then has the right of administrative appeal and, if that is lost, the right to file a court action, against the attorney general, for a declaratory judgment of citizenship.

In the case of a denial by the consulate of a travel document, for the child still in Hong Kong, on the ground the consular officer does not think the applicant is a citizen, the father's attorney here can appeal to the Panel Board of the State Department.

If the Panel Board rejects the claim, the attorney can then file an action in the Federal Court in the district where the father resides, against the Secretary of State, asking for a declaratory judgment of citizenship. A certified copy of the complaint is sent to the consul in Hong Kong with the request that the consul direct the child to file an application for a certificate of identity, which would enable him to come to the United States and appear at his trial. (If he loses the trial, then he is deportable.)

At this juncture, the consular officer conducts a complete, new, independent investigation. Then he can refuse a certificate of identity on the grounds that the boy, through his father's attorney, has not brought the court action in good faith, or that the boy is not the person he claims to be.

The attorney can appeal from this decision to the Panel Board of the State Department, but this time the appeal must go *through the consular officer in Hong Kong.* If the Panel Board also rejects this appeal, the attorney can get a court order to compel the State Department to issue the certificate of identity. But the State Department, although a defendant in a legal proceeding, may ignore this court injunction, as it has done in the past. Under Public Law 414, of course, by placing the whole matter of citizenship claims abroad in the hands of consular officers, no such court action is even permissible.

Perhaps the oddest aspect of this whole procedure is the fact that an appeal from an adverse consular decision must be taken *through* the consular officer.

Chapter

17   It is an established principle set down by the Founding Fathers that in the United States the power of those who govern stems from the governed. The American people do not cotton to the idea of little men wielding autocratic power. It goes against the democratic grain. Indeed, too much authority lends itself to abuse and corruption. But its most common outgrowth is arrogance—what Shakespeare called "the insolence of office."

The story of what happened to the Orloffs is a clear example—unhappily, by no means rare—of how the uncurbed power vested in underlings of our Foreign Service breeds an insolence of office.

Alexander S. Orloff, a Russian corporation lawyer, was once legal adviser to the Polish Embassy in Moscow and counsel for Igerussko, the Russian branch of the I. G. Farbenindustrie of Germany. In 1930, when the Soviets decided to liquidate the so-called New Economic Policy, Orloff sensed that his connection with foreign capitalism placed his life in jeopardy. Denied an exit passport, he escaped to Manchuria with his wife, Sabine, and their son, Vsevolod. From there they went to Shanghai.

Eventually, they were forced to flee Communists again, this time the Chinese Reds. They took refuge, as stateless persons, at the International Refugee Organization camp on the small island of Tubabao off the southeastern tip of Samar, the Philippines.

It is important to bear in mind that Orloff has affidavits attesting his good moral character and his long opposition to Communism.

On November 9, 1950, the elder Orloffs were interviewed at Tubabao by a pair of American vice consuls, whom we shall call Mr. Brown and Mr. Jones. Although the Orloffs were not admitted until all other appointments of the day had been disposed of, shortly after 9 P.M., and had a considerable wait while the consular officers dined— a small inconvenience, but indicative of the treatment to come—the refugees foresaw no difficulties. After all, their son, who was present at the interview, had already been granted a preference visa because he possessed special talents our military was eager to put to use, and he had just as eagerly offered his services.

Let Alexander Orloff describe that interview, as excerpted from a sworn statement he made shortly afterward:

> From the beginning their [the vice consuls'] attitude was hostile and arrogant. After a few words directed at my son, Mr. Brown asked my wife what was her profession. She replied that she was an actress.
>
> "Ah, so," said Mr. Brown ironically, burlesquing a cabaret dancer, "a night club dancer."
>
> "Oh, no," protested my wife, "I am a dramatic actress."
>
> "In what plays do you act? Shakespeare? Do you play Hamlet or Ophelia?"

This sounded like a joke. Hamlet is a man's part and Ophelia, according to the play, a sixteen-year-old girl, whilst my wife is a lady 57 years of age.

Now the interrogation turned to me and Mr. Brown's tone changed from irony to arrogance.

"When did you renounce your Soviet passport?" he asked.

"I never had a Soviet passport abroad."

"This is a lie. We know everything. When did you renounce your Soviet passport?"

"Excuse me, but here are my documents—"

"I don't care about your documents. We know everything. When did you renounce your Soviet passport?"

He shouted, pounding the desk with his fist. Nevertheless, I took out my documents from the briefcase and put them in front of him. All my emigrant papers proved to be in perfect order. Amongst them was also a *Carte D'Identite* issued to me by the French police at Shanghai. Seeing this gray book Mr. Brown grabbed it.

"Aha, you are the holder of a valid French passport and you are hiding it."

It cost me a lot of effort to convince him that the document had been issued to a Russian emigrant. But from then on accusations started flowing incessantly.

"You are a collaborator—you worked with the Japanese."

"I beg your pardon. I was arrested by the Japanese *gendarmerie* upon investigation of a certain Howens (a Japanese agent) and was under surveillance until the end of the war. Here is my statement."

"So? You know Howens. In other words, you worked together with him?"

"How could I have been working with Howens when he was my enemy and it was due to him I was arrested?"

This unexpectedly hostile tone of Mr. Brown, all his

shouting and pounding of his desk, affected my wife so that she felt faint and asked for some water.

Mr. Brown replied: "We have not water for such as you."

Now my file was taken up by Mr. Jones.

Mr. Jones said: "You were a lawyer in Moscow? That means you are a Communist."

"I never was a Communist."

"In the U.S.S.R. only party members can be lawyers. Therefore you are a Communist."

"In my time the greatest majority of lawyers did not belong to the party. I never sympathized with Communism. I was the lawyer of the Polish Embassy and of other foreign concerns. Please look at the letter from Mr. Foss, the former manager of Igerussko, where I worked."

Mr. Jones said: "So you were connected with the IG? Tell me the date of your joining the Nazi Party."

"How could I have been a member of the Nazi Party when I am Russian and not German? I was connected with the IG from 1925 to 1930 when hardly anyone knew about the Nazi Party."

"No, you are a Nazi. Tell me the date when you joined the Nazi Party."

All the questions of Mr. Jones were accompanied by his pounding the table, shouts and continuous scowls. My wife's nerves could not hold out any longer. Getting up, she made several steps towards the entrance and fainted near the door to the corridor. Neither one of the investigators made even the slightest move to help her.

The cup of my patience also overflowed. Why this constant flow of accusation, completely groundless and absurd? Why this tone, worthy of a third degree of a criminal caught red-handed?

"Gentlemen," I said, "I see that you do not trust me.

Under these circumstances, I have nothing further to do here. I am leaving. I don't want anything from you."

With these words I gathered from the table the documents and started to put them in my briefcase. At this Mr. Jones jumped up and grabbed hold of my files.

"No, you will leave all this here," he said.

The file contained all my documents and intimate correspondence, but to tear it out of his hands would have given him the opportunity to say that it contained something incriminating, so I let go. Triumphantly Mr. Jones threw the file on the desk.

"No tricks, baby," he said, shaking his finger in front of my face. (By age, Mr. Jones could have been my son.)

Thereupon, Mr. Jones delivered a resounding speech on the subject of traitors who want to stab his country in the back. He shouted that before allowing such a person as I to enter the United States, he would rather bash in my head.

"Get out!" he finished.

Completely overwhelmed, I left the office. On the open space in front of the consulate my wife was lying. Dr. Tucker was trying to revive her. Dozens of excited people milled around. Without difficulty they could hear the interview as the investigators did not spare their lungs. Like a flock of sheep at the appearance of a wild beast, the crowd shied away when I came out. Who could this be who was treated like that by the consular officials? My good name was smeared in that evening.

During my life I had been arrested several times by political police, twice in the U.S.S.R. and finally by the Japanese *gendarmerie* in Shanghai. But never did I feel so degraded and insulted as after this interview at the American consulate on Tubabao. I had entered the consulate with reverence just like a temple. I came by the right given me by the American people. I was insulted, and kicked out like a dog . . . Mr. Brown and Mr. Jones cannot but admit they transgressed all bounds of propriety. After all, they are members of the American consular staff and not members of the Gestapo who have to make me pay for their errors and who have to destroy me to save their face.

A month later Orloff was summoned to another interview. An armed Filipino in military uniform was stationed at the door. Orloff, in his sworn statement, relates that experience:

A Filipino *gendarme* in the office of an American consular official during an interview. What can this mean? Are the interviewers afraid of some sort of excess on my part? Or do they intend to provoke an excess, thus to shut the door of America to me illegally?

Only Mr. Jones, apparently for reasons of scaring me, acted like some sort of phantom, shook his fist and made horrid grimaces. It was clear after the first words that my position was hopeless. They were absolutely not interested in the latter period of my life—twenty years of life as an emigrant. Their whole attention was directed at my activity in the U.S.S.R. up to 1930.

From the questions I made two deductions. First, that they were completely unfamiliar with the legal and common aspects of life in the U.S.S.R. from 1923 to 1930. This was the period of the so-called New Economic Policy, when private capital was permitted and the whole aspect of life under a cloak of socialism bore a quasi-bourgeoise character. Knowing only the present position, they therefore did not understand how such a position could exist altogether in the U.S.S.R. Secondly, that they were firing into the dark, for they have neither grounds nor any possible material which would justify their accusations.

Mr. Brown asked: "What were you doing in Vladivostok in 1921, I think, and in 1925?"

"I was never in that city until 1930."

"In those years you were in Vladivostok and were engaged there in pro-Communist work."

"This is not so."

"No, this is the truth. A person here in camp can certify to it."

"Bring me face to face with this person, and I will prove to you that he is lying."

This request was left without answer. Not only here in camp but such a person could not exist in the whole world.

Finally the interview reached its culminating point. Mr. Brown started to formulate the accusation. As a convicting document, I was confronted with my own biography which I had voluntarily presented and which I was absolutely certain would open the door to me of any non-Communist country.

In one of the paragraphs it said that with a change in the policy of the Soviet government, prominent employees of foreign concerns were arrested, tried and confined in concentration camps. Being afraid of similar persecution, I was forced to flee abroad. Previously in the same biography I had mentioned that I had been arrested by the GPU (political police) in 1921 and 1927.

Basing himself upon these happenings, Mr. Brown bravely erected the following theory: Since in 1930 I had not been arrested together with the others but fled abroad, therefore I *must have had* some secret connections with the political police. These connections *must have* developed as a price for release from arrest in 1921 and 1927. This means that I *must have* been a Soviet agent and therefore *must have* been giving the Soviet government secret information about the activity of the Polish

Embassy in Moscow and about foreign concerns whose legal adviser I was.

Upon hearing this, I took up my file which had been just returned to me and which contained documents which would have completely disproved all these theories of Mr. Brown's. However, I was very rudely stopped.

Mr. Brown said: "We have no interest in your documents. We have already seen them and know all about them."

"Excuse me, but I have letters both from the Polish Embassy and Igerussko, in which they thank me for my services. I could not have received such a letter had I been conducting treasonable work against them."

"You betrayed them."

The Polish Embassy where I had worked for seven years and which expressed its gratitude for my valuable assistance was betrayed by me? I had betrayed the IG where I had worked for five years and where my services were very much appreciated? Only after twenty-five years were two gentlemen on the island of Tubabao able, and that based on my own biography, to make the discovery that I had been a Soviet agent and a traitor.

Mr. Brown said: "You were accused of being a paid Soviet agent in the U.S.S.R."

"No. How can I admit that I am guilty?"

"No explanations. You are not in court. Yes or no?"

"No."

And so came up the psychological moment for which apparently the Filipino *gendarme* had been prepared.

Mr. Brown said three times, looking me straight in the eyes: "You lie! You lie! You lie!"

It is hard to imagine a more severe insult. However, I controlled myself and did not fall for his provocation. I only asked him the following question, "Tell me, Mr.

Brown, how you can accuse me of anything without basing it on any proof?"

Mr. Brown said: "That is our right. The burden of defense is yours."

This ended the second interview.

Mr. and Mrs. Orloff were refused visas.

Their son, by now in the United States, retained the San Francisco law firm of Jackson & Hertogs. Late in 1951 Attorney Joseph S. Hertogs received word from the State Department, in response to his request for reconsideration, that it had no objection to reopening the case.

But the American consul general at Manila had an objection. He informed Hertogs: "It may be pointed out that this is not the equivalent of requesting the Embassy to reconsider the case. Under the law, the responsibility of issuing or rejecting a visa lies with the consular officer in charge of visas in the office where the application is made.

"In the case under consideration, it should be remembered that, despite the unfortunate circumstances involved in the Orloffs' interview . . . their [the vice consuls'] decision was not made lightly or hastily . . . It is not believed that any useful purpose may be served considering the case further."

And that was that.

The elder Orloffs were denied entry to the United States presumably for the security reason that Alexander Orloff had practiced law in Moscow a quarter of a century ago. Yet their son was admitted for permanent residence. Furthermore, he holds a position of a confidential nature with our armed forces.

While they were still on the island of Tubabao—still hopeful they might make it to America—Mrs. Orloff received a letter from her son's commanding officer, a lieutenant colonel. The letter said, in part:

"By his unusual initiative and ability, your fine boy Vsevolod has earned a promotion . . . I would like to extend my congratulations and best wishes to you, his mother.

"Your son is a part of a mighty force which, it is hoped, will help maintain peace for our country. His job is to help preserve these United States and their representative form of government for us and for our children. You have every right to be proud of him for the fine job he is performing in the defense of our country."

The Orloffs were welcomed to Brazil. Whether they will ever be able to come to the country their son is serving so admirably appears problematical.

Such is the effect of placing so much authority in the hands of little men. But arrogance is not the only harvest, for absolute power also offers a fertile soil for corruption. A person who lived in Hong Kong a few years ago told me: "You could buy a passport or visa there as easily as buying a beefsteak."

John Wayne Williams, former American vice consul at Hong Kong, is now serving a penitentiary term. He admitted taking bribes and gifts totaling nearly $10,000 for "expediting visas to Chinese to visit or transit the United States en route to some other country."

Charlie Liu, a Chinese of Hong Kong, came to the University of California on a student visa after the war.

While here he married a Chinese-American citizen of San Francisco. They had two children before he returned to Hong Kong upon completion of his studies.

He was denied even a visitor's visa by the consulate in Hong Kong to come back and see his American family. The reason? A consular officer informally told him: "Since your family is in the United States, you might want to stay there."

Liu, understandably anxious to see his family, greased a palm, as the saying goes, with $1,000. He got a visitor's visa—from the American consulate in Bangkok, where he had never been in his life. While in San Francisco he applied to Immigration for adjustment of his status to permanent residence, on a showing of economic detriment to his American family. He was questioned about the Bangkok-issued visa and he frankly related how, in desperation, he had come by it. He was served with a deportation warrant. If deported, he will be forever barred from returning to his family.

A similar problem faced a Chinese in Hong Kong who had an American wife and child in San Francisco. It so happened that he had urgent business here. These were the steps—like moves in chess—he took:

He sent for his wife and child. When they arrived in Hong Kong, he applied for a temporary visa, stating: "Look, my family is here in Hong Kong, so naturally I won't want to stay in the United States." He got the visa, came to San Francisco, transacted his business, returned to Hong Kong, sent his family back to San Francisco.

Chapter

18   Immigration officials are also subject to
the laws of human nature, and in this field it seems that
men with great power can be equally susceptible to en-
ticement. One, at least, was.

In the following account, the identity of the people involved is withheld for obvious reasons.

A friend of mine—let's call him Mr. Harley—was an international lawyer of New York in the late 'thirties and
early 'forties. A man of great compassion, he was distressed
by the plight of Jews under Nazism. At the solicitation of
relatives and friends in the United States, he made frequent trips to Germany to help pave an exit for Jews in
trouble. He boldly talked the head of the *politzei* into releasing a number of prominent Jews from concentration
camps and permitting them to leave Germany—some of
whom later rendered invaluable service to our War Department.

It often happened that Mr. Harley encountered greater
difficulty getting these refugees into the United States—
even those who later materially aided our national defense

—than he had encountered getting them out of Hitler's clutches.

"The callous brutality with which the Immigration Service treated many of those who sought refuge here is almost beyond belief," he says. "And the worst of it is that in the majority of such cases there is nothing one can do, for the service hides behind the screen of 'ministerial discretion,' or else refuses to give any reason at all for its decisions. When too hotly pressed, it has even used *agents provocateur* to 'get' those who oppose it."

By chance, Mr. Harley found a way to get around this ministerial discretion.

"I was told by an astute Washingtonian that one could readily get difficult cases through the bureau by retaining the right 'fixer,' " he reveals. "In a dozen difficult cases I simply retained him, where the applicants could afford his fee, to 'arrange' matters."

Mr. Harley tells of one particularly tough case. It goes back to a day in Paris, in 1939, when a friend brought a woman to see him at the Hotel Crillon. This woman was a Jew with a German passport and a French visa. They talked briefly and Mr. Harley gave her his card, stating, "If you are ever in New York and need help, call me."

He thought no more of the incident until one day many months later he received a telephone call from Ellis Island.

"On the phone," he relates, "was this woman I had met in Paris. She spoke only German and French, but she was hysterical in both languages. She begged me to come to Ellis Island at once. Ordinarily, I would have sent an assistant, but she seemed so desperate I went myself."

This is what he learned: The woman, sensing the imminent outbreak of war, had boarded a ship for New York. She was on the Atlantic when war did break out, and France cancelled the visas of all German nationals. She was taken into custody by immigration officials in New York and lodged at Ellis Island, then ordered excluded—to be sent back to Germany.

Three times her case—meritorious as it was—had been turned down on appeals made by the Hebrew Immigrant Aid Society (HIAS). And now there was no hope. If returned to Germany, she would most certainly have met her doom in the gas chambers of Buchenwald or Dachau, for both the crime of fleeing to the United States with more than the handful of marks permitted, and the more heinous crime—in the eyes of the Nazis—of being a Jew.

In her desperation, she had remembered the American who had offered to help her that day in the Hotel Crillon.

Mr. Harley, who usually took a modest fee, sometimes none at all, for his services in such cases, inquired as to her financial standing, with the fixer in mind. She produced evidence that she had a substantial sum on deposit in a New York bank.

"I'll see what can be done for you," he said. (In none of these cases, of course, did he ever reveal the procedure whereby he won the individual's release.)

Mr. Harley went to Washington immediately and saw the fixer. "This is a pretty tough case," he warned.

The fixer grinned. "Then it'll be a pretty tough fee." (He never worried about his ability to fix a case; in fact, he often borrowed against future fees.)

Mr. Harley shrewdly withheld the size of the woman's bank account, else the fixer might have made the price tougher. As it was, the fee came to only a few hundred dollars.

Within several days the exclusion order was cancelled, and the woman admitted into the United States.

Even Mr. Harley was astonished. Several months later, as he was negotiating another difficult case, he asked the fixer how in heaven's name he had gotten that earlier tough case cleared so quickly.

"Easy," boasted the fixer with a chuckle and a sweeping gesture. "Just a lavish dinner party for a high official and his wife—plus the gift of a beautiful Japanese silk kimono to the wife!"

At that, the fixer was put to an annoying inconvenience. Pondering what sort of gift he could present to the high immigration official's wife this time, he recalled her ecstatic raving over a Japanese silk kimono he had brought back as a souvenir from a trip to the Philippines some years previous. He had later sold the kimono. He rued it now, because he had to spend the better part of a day scouring Washington's shops until he found a kimono that was almost a duplicate of the souvenir she had exclaimed over.

Says Mr. Harley, still appalled by the devious course justice must sometimes pursue: "Such an 'appeal' was far more potent than all the pleas of HIAS."

Whose is the moral guilt in this case—the refugee who provided the money, the counsellor who paid the fixer, the fixer himself, or the high official of the Immigration Service who sold his favors for a price? The refugee was buying her freedom, even life itself. The counsellor was resorting to a last desperate measure to save this refugee and others like her from a frightful fate, the horror of which was later to shock the world. Nor can the fixer be wholly condemned. Censurable as his role may seem, he nevertheless was the instrument whereby these innocent lives were spared.

But what of this responsible immigration officer, who for a paltry gift sold the freedom of America to people already entitled to it by virtue of flight from a death-dealing tyrant?

Chapter

19 One Texas-bright day early in 1949 the
Reverend Julias Dworaczyk, a Catholic priest, visited the
Bexar County jail at San Antonio. He overheard a chance
remark about "that Polack in the back cell."

Curious, being of Polish ancestry himself, the priest in-
vestigated. In a sunless cell block of the ancient jail he discovered Zygmunt Adamusia, a 32-year-old Polish refugee.
Scrawny and pallid, the prisoner had a long red beard and
wore grimy, tattered clothes. He had the stare of a man too
long in dismal confinement.

Zygmunt Adamusia had been behind bars for thirteen
months, with no sun, no news, no exercise, no attention
and, worst of all, with no regard for due process of law.
His jailers, frankly bewildered, did not know what to do
with him. An immigration officer had brought in the Pole
one day and told the sheriff's men to hold him. And they
had been holding him ever since. (This practice of lodg-
ing a man in a county jail on a technical hold-for-immigra-
tion charge, and without bond, is common.)

Ordinarily, you must go through Immigration channels
to visit such a prisoner. But the priest, in his deep concern,

forgot about channels. He learned these details: Adamusia, as a Free Pole, had fought with the Allied Forces in Italy during World War II. After the war he went to England and eventually journeyed to Venezuela, afraid to go back to Poland because the Communists had taken over. In Venezuela he was told that he could join the United States Army, and he came up through Mexico and crossed the border into Texas without a visa. Immigration authorities picked him up in San Antonio, put him in jail and apparently forgot about him.

Father Dworaczyk took the story to the San Antonio *Evening News*. "This man is slowly losing weight and becoming a little peculiar from such long confinement," he told an *Evening News* reporter. "It's difficult to find out anything. The federal authorities seem to be just indifferent to the whole thing."

Just how indifferent came to light when the *Evening News* reporter telephoned William A. Whalen, then district director of immigration at San Antonio.

Whalen appeared startled when the reporter asked for information about the prisoner. "You mean he's been in jail here that long?" he asked.

"Yes," the reporter replied.

"Well, it certainly isn't one of our cases, is it?"

The reporter said he understood it was. "This *is* the Immigration Department, isn't it?"

"Yes, but I don't know anything about him. Maybe he's been sentenced to jail."

"No. He's booked 'Hold for Immigration.'"

"Well, what's his name?" Whalen asked. "I'll take a look at the records and see what it's all about."

Whalen came back on the line in a few minutes and said he had located the record, but he refused to reveal any of it. He rolled an iron curtain down on Adamusia and flatly rejected the reporter's request to interview the Pole. Whalen explained that subordinates had handled the case and he had simply forgotten all about Adamusia being in jail. And he blandly passed off the long overdue due process in the refugee's unremembered confinement with the comment:

"This fellow admits coming in from Mexico illegally. If a court found him guilty and sentenced him to prison, we'd still have to deport him when he got out."

Then why had he not been deported before this?

Whalen explained that the Polish consul general in Chicago would not authorize Adamusia's return to his native land. And so: "The whole thing rests with the Polish authorities. We can't do a thing till they let him return."

Maury Maverick, the former Congressman, now practicing law in San Antonio, took a different view. He considered the Pole's confinement as both unconscionable and unconstitutional—a feeling intensified by the shock he experienced when he first beheld the unkempt prisoner in the jail.

Maverick spent a few weeks looking into the case. He learned that the Pole had been given what he describes with quotes as a "hearing." This was a hearing, under the procedure of the previous immigration law, by a Board of Special Inquiry, made up of two immigration officers and a stenographer, each with a vote. "The vote," says Maverick, "is always unanimous."

When next Maverick visited the Pole in the county jail, he was pleased to find the publicity had produced one salutary effect: Adamusia was clean-shaven, he was wearing new clothes, and he was eating chocolate bars. But he was strangely reticent—until, upon persistent questioning, he explained that he had been warned he would get five years in prison if he talked to the lawyer. That really stirred Maverick's dander, and he vowed to get the Pole out into the open air.

When the local immigration authorities refused to release the Pole on bond, Maverick wrote to Congressman John Lesinski: "I have Polish people here who are willing to take care of this man. He can get a job. He has not even seen sunshine during these [by now] fourteen months, and according to my viewpoint, it is 'cruel and inhuman punishment' without due process of law. The Federals say he will run away. Where will he run to?

"Urge the immigration authorities to release him on parole, and I promise to do all the legal work free and also get a sponsorship of several very respectable people in this county."

Maverick postscripted: "P.S. My interest in this is simply to get this man in the sunshine. It isn't right to keep him there all this time."

Immigration authorities in Washington refused to parole him "for security reasons," despite the fact that

Maverick says there was preponderant evidence to show the Polish refugee was anti-Communist.

Maverick took the last avenue of hope. He filed a petition in Federal Court for a writ of habeas corpus on the grounds Adamusia had been held too long in jail without due process and that he would be subjected to "torture, imprisonment or death due to political considerations, if he returned to Poland."

Before the federal judge could issue the writ, the Pole was whisked out of the court's jurisdiction—destination unknown.

"This was clearly to evade any judicial right due Adamusia, especially of habeas corpus, or any outside aid, or the usual rights of a human being," said the dismayed Maverick.

This brings up the question of justice under our immigration laws. Congressman Walter, co-author of the 1952 Act, says "the new law also provides that in every deportation case a hearing is mandatory and appeal to the courts is permitted."

Yes and no. The new act does make provision for a hearing, but hearings, such as they are, have always been the practice in deportation cases. The Supreme Court had held that the requirement for a fair hearing was implicit in the Constitution—that *due process under the Fifth Amendment applied to all persons in the United States, whether citizen or alien.*

"Such a 'hearing' as set forth in the immigration law means nothing," says Maverick. "It is not in court; it is by persons all decided in advance. After a 'hearing,' Immigration can continue to hold."

An appeal to the courts is permitted? That is still open to question. The only appeal specifically provided for is *an administrative appeal within the Justice Department.* And that, according to every tradition of the Declaration of Independence and the Bill of Rights and common fairness, is widely considered among the legal fraternity as a denial of human rights.

The congressional conference report on the bill that became Public Law 414 stated that "The safeguard of judicial procedure is afforded the alien in both exclusion and deportation proceedings." But, as the President's Commission pointed out, it does not explain or clearly indicate just how.

The act refers to judicial review only in cryptic language —an oblique reference in Section 242 granting the attorney general six months to effect an alien's departure from the date of a final order of deportation "or, if judicial review is had, then from the date of the final order of the court." In contrast to that obscurity, the act states definitely that "in any case in which an alien is ordered deported . . . the decision of the attorney general shall be final." And the Supreme Court has inferred from such language in former immigration statutes that the attorney general and his administrative officers are authorized to function "without judicial intervention."

Since Public Law 414 went into effect, the United States Court of Appeals for the District of Columbia, with a divided bench, has ruled that Section 10 of the Administrative Procedure Act of 1946 applies to the new immigration law. This section of the APA provides for judicial review of administrative decisions if statutes do not deny it. The appellate court based its ruling on the oblique reference in Section 242 of the McCarran Act—*i.e.*, "if judicial review is had"—and a statement by Senator McCarran during the Senate debate on his bill that the Administrative Procedure Act was applicable.

The Supreme Court has not yet been heard from on this newly raised point. But it did rule on the same question under the previous immigration law—that Section 10 of the APA was *not* applicable. In fact, the Supreme Court held that habeas corpus remained the only procedure by which an alien may challenge a deportation order in the courts. It pointed out that for a quarter of a century the high court had held that when Congress made the administrative decision final, "the authority of the courts to review the decision of the executive officers was taken away."

"We hold that deportation orders remain immune to direct attack," the Supreme Court said. ". . . The function of the courts has always been limited to the enforcement of due process requirements [habeas corpus]."

Just what was the intent of Congress in this regard? If Congress intended to provide for judicial review in deportation cases why did it not clearly say so? If Congress intended to make the provisions of the Administrative Procedure Act applicable, again why did it not clearly say so? Why, instead, did it retain the provision that a decision of the attorney general "shall be final"?

Let us go back to the debate that preceded enactment of Public Law 414.

On April 24, 1952, Congressman George Meader, Republican of Michigan, offered three amendments which he said would "seek to restore the right of judicial review of administrative decisions." His third amendment, in particular, was designed to "strike language which indicates that the decision of the attorney general shall be final."

"A basic principle of constitutional law is involved here," said Congressman Meader. "Administrative agencies have been encroaching upon the legislative function and likewise upon the judicial function. Here they seek to be free from supervision and review by the courts of the United States. I say we ought to say plainly and unequivocally that administrative decisions are subject to judicial review. This amendment will make clear that that judicial review is available. We should not leave it up to a tenuous interpretation of some Supreme Court decision."

Congressman Clare E. Hoffman, also a Michigan Republican, asked his colleague: "Are the people for whom the gentleman is seeking this benefit or privilege citizens?"

Congressman Meader replied: "Of course not. A citizen cannot be deported."

Congressman Hoffman asked: "Then do you think those who are not citizens have the right to appeal to the courts and go on up to the highest court?"

Congressman Meader replied: "I think that an alien in this country, who has lived his life here and established a family, and acquired property, has rights which should be determined by a court, and not by an arbitrary bureaucratic official."

Congressman Meader's amendments were killed.

True, both Senator McCarran and Congressman Walter insist the Administrative Procedure Act is applicable to their immigration act. During the debate on May 22, 1952, Senator McCarran assured his collegues that his bill "makes the Administrative Procedure Act applicable insofar as the administration of the bill is concerned."

But that very same day Senator Wayne Morse, Oregon Independent, offered an amendment to bring the McCarran bill "under the provisions of the Administrative Procedure Act" in keeping, he said, with the recommendation of the American Bar Association. Senator Morse's amendment also clearly provided for judicial review in both exclusion and deportation cases. As the McCarran bill then stood, Senator Morse said, it denied "the right to a review of the decision of the administrative officer by a court."

Senator Morse's amendment was killed.

The ruling of the United States Court of Appeals for the District of Columbia, interpreting the McCarran Act as granting the right of judicial review, applies only to that district. Appellate courts in other districts may take a different view, and so might the Supreme Court if and when the question again comes before it. Elsewhere in the country, therefore, the alien's only recourse, once ordered deported, might be a petition for a writ of habeas corpus, which is not synonymous with a judicial review. Once in custody, the alien derives this limited right from the Fifth

Amendment. And in such a proceeding, the court simply determines whether the alien has had a fair hearing.

And there's the rub. Lawyers have long decried the unfairness of hearing procedure under immigration rules. These rules, they say, are patently made by immigration authorities to suit themselves. The result is that the alien, in a petition for a writ of habeas corpus, simply asks the court to consider whether the hearing was *fair* under an *unfair* procedure. Lawyers say it doesn't make sense, either legal or common.

Even if the alien wins in his habeas corpus action, Immigration can hold another hearing, and another, and another, involving double, triple, quadruple jeopardy.

"They try him again and again, on the same charges," says Maverick, "until this Royal Mounted gets its man. Immigration officials are not bad men. They are simply Javerts—like Javert in *Les Miserables*, who was so conscientious he always got his man—and *always* got his man. It's the law—a bad one, which should be repealed or greatly amended—and it's administered with a cold implacability never equaled in the history of America.

"Our Immigration Service is the greatest bureaucracy on earth. Stricken by the McCarthy terror of Communism, it looks upon all aliens as wicked people and constantly fights them. Unfortunately, the result appears like the same disregard for human rights that the Soviets practice. Unfortunately, above all, the Congress has written a law which gives immigration officers little chance to show any mercy."

The trouble lies in the refusal of Immigration—blessed

by the McCarran Act—to adhere to the Administrative
Procedure Act of 1946, which decreed that hearing officers, or examiners, must be divorced from investigative
or prosecuting functions. It also decreed that hearing officers should be men with legal training, appointed by the
Civil Service Commission and answerable to that body.

The most important agency which failed to comply with
the APA was the Immigration Service, which continued
the practice whereby the hearing officer also served as
prosecutor. (It used to be a three-in-one deal: arresting
officer, prosecutor and judge all wrapped up in the same
person.) Worse, the President's Commission deplored the
fact that "approximately 60 per cent of the hearing officers
do not have college degrees or legal training," which it felt
essential to their "capacity to deal justly with human rights
and aspirations."

In 1950 the Supreme Court held that such a prosecutor-
judge setup was far from ideal as a safeguard of a fair
hearing and ordered Immigration to comply with the provisions of the Administrative Procedure Act. Congress
promptly nullified that injunction by attaching a rider to
the next appropriation bill, exempting Immigration from
the provisions of the APA.

Apparently perturbed by the shocked protests that
greeted this action, the sponsors of the 1952 Act came up
with what they happily called a "fair" hearing procedure.
Congressman Walter told his colleagues during the House
debate that the new procedure "reinstated" the Supreme
Court order. However, the APA still does not apply because Public Law 414 specifically states that the new pro-

cedure shall be "the sole and exclusive procedure for determining the deportability of an alien . . ." And Senator Morse, in offering an amendment that would have brought the McCarran Act under the APA, stated that the 1952 Act "does not provide for independent hearing examiners in deportation cases as required by the Supreme Court."

The 1950 Supreme Court decision regarding deportation hearings cited the report of the Secretary of Labor's Committee on Administrative Procedure in 1940: "A genuinely impartial hearing, conducted with critical detachment, is psychologically improbable if not impossible, when the presiding officer has at once the responsibility of appraising the strength of the case and of seeking to make it as strong as possible. Nor is complete divorce between investigation and hearing possible so long as the presiding inspector has the duty himself of assembling and presenting the results of the investigation."

Professors Louis J. Jaffe and Henry M. Hart, Jr., of the Harvard Law School, told the President's Commission: "To say, as Section 242 (b) does, that 'no special inquiry officer shall conduct a proceeding in any case . . . in which he shall have participated (except as provided in this subsection) in prosecuting functions,' and simultaneously to allow the officer to be given responsibility for building the record against the alien, is discreditable double talk."

They also urged that APA safeguards be applied to exclusion as well as deportation hearings, because: "The attitude toward the immigrant should be one of friendliness and welcome, a recognition of his tremendous interest in the transaction, of the vital interest of his American relatives, friends, and sponsors, and of the interest of the country. Once he had made the determination to come here, to pull up stakes, to invest in transportation for himself and his family, it is cruel to send him back unless he has received an unimpeachable hearing."

Their views that the 1952 Act was unsound insofar as it superseded the APA were concurred in by the American Bar Association.

This brief excerpt from a recent hearing reveals how the prosecutor-judge role works in actual practice. The hearing officer was cross-examining a distraught woman fighting deportation to a satellite country where she feared imprisonment.

Hearing Officer: "How much did you pay [implying a bribe] to get over here?"

She: "I didn't pay anything."

Hearing Officer: "Oh, come now, don't give me any of that!"

An aspect of the law that has already proved unworkable is the provision that the Immigration Service, in an appellate court action arising out of a naturalization case, must present the views of both the commissioner and the designated examiner, where they disagree. Jack Wasserman, Washington immigration lawyer, tells of a case before the U. S. Court of Appeals for the Southern District of New York wherein the Government prosecutor had to defend the views of the commissioner, who recommended naturalization, and the examiner, who was opposed. Says Wasserman: "The United States attorney was reprimanded because he didn't have his brief in, and his explanation to the court was that he was in a quandary; he didn't know which side he was on; he didn't know whether he would have to speak out of both sides of his mouth."

The attorney general can, and does, detain persons indefinitely without a hearing and without an announced reason—a right upheld by the Supreme Court. Congress bestowed this power on the attorney general and, at least on one occasion, was disconcerted by it. This was in the case of Ellen Knauff, the German war bride held at Ellis Island for three years. When she had been in detention a year and a half, members of the House Judiciary Committee, upon receipt of numerous protests, made an inquiry.

Congress Emanuel Celler told the House on April 24, 1952: "[The committee members] exhaustively went into this case, and took the position, very properly and logically, that Mrs. Knauff should be admitted. There was no reason under the sun why she should have been excluded. We then communicated with the attorney general and told him about our deliberations and our judgment. The attorney general utterly disregarded the opinion of the Judiciary Committee of this august body and said, in effect, he did not care what the Judiciary Committee would judge in this matter; that he was going to hold her."

When immigration authorities do release a person on bond or parole they impose penalties and restrictions *prior to a final finding*. This has been attacked as far too broad a power.

A man thus freed—on bail often exceeding that set by a court in a criminal action—can be prosecuted in a criminal court if he fails to comply with any of these administrative restrictions: He must not leave the city or county of his residence without applying for written permission, even if it's for a day's outing. He must furnish a complete financial statement every month—something not even the Internal Revenue Bureau can require. He must not associate with a person of "low character" (what if there's one in the office where he works?) or "frequent places where criminals congregate" (the streets, theaters, county fairs?). He must not change jobs unless he gets an okay, nor change addresses, without notifying Immigration.

The law provides that courts shall have authority to review determinations denying bail in deportation cases only upon "a conclusive showing in habeas corpus proceedings that the attorney general is not proceeding with . . . reasonable dispatch." The President's Commission viewed this provision as apparently attempting to preclude the courts from considering whether denials of bail have been arbitrary or illegal.

"Again we have habeas corpus as the only judicial recourse," says one immigration lawyer. "And a man must be in custody to take that step. Why should a person have to surrender his freedom to gain judicial relief—to regain his freedom? It amounts to the same thing."

Even when a person *is* in custody, he may be denied even that relief. Such was the situation with Zygmunt Adamusia, the Polish refugee held in jail fourteen months and then whisked out of the area when his counsel sought a writ of habeas corpus.

It was later learned that Adamusia was flown out of San Antonio by special plane to New York, and there removed to Ellis Island, and there to await deportation to "Venezuela, if practicable, otherwise, to Poland." For all any ordinary citizen may find out, Adamusia may still be at Ellis Island. The Immigration Service has always been extremely reluctant about releasing any information, even to lawyers, unless it suits a purpose of the service. This practice of secretly imprisoning people is a stock-in-trade of the immigration watchdogs.

There are certain notorious exceptions to the secrecy rule. When the Immigration Service has an ulterior design, it will rush to the press with information. In such cases, the motive is patently to stigmatize a person before he is given a hearing. This was demonstrated in the case of Pasquale Sciortino.

Sciortino jumped ship at New York in 1948, a political refugee from Italy. He had been a leader in a movement to restore Sicily to its ancient independence. His father was assassinated by the Fascists because he favored democracy. The *Movimento Independista Siciliano*, or Free Sicily Movement, was both anti-Fascist and anti-Communist. For his part in it, Sciortino was tortured by the Italian Communists. They put him on the *cassetti*, a medieval stretching rack; they slashed his chest (the scars remain) and poured vinegar on the raw wounds; they nauseated him with forced quantities of salt water. Immigration authorities did not deny that this was so.

Moreover, Sciortino's adherence to democratic principles was shown by the fact that, when he was a reluctant conscript in the Italian army during the last war, he deserted to fight alongside the Americans.

After his flight to the United States, Sciortino was tried and convicted *in absentia* in Italy—a procedure unknown to our jurisprudence—on political charges masked as other crimes, according to his counsel, our same Maury Maverick.

Salvatore Guiliano, the "Robin Hood" bandit of Sicily, forced Sciortino into a midnight marriage with Guiliano's sister. Documentary evidence reveals the irregular nature of that ceremony. Some time after his arrival in the United States, Sciortino said, he learned that the marriage had been annulled. (It wasn't.) He then married a Michigan girl, and they have one child.

Sciortino, well-educated, was a disc jockey for a radio station in a Western city for a while, then joined the United States Air Force. He was stationed at Lackland Air Force Base, San Antonio, when immigration authorities took him into custody in August of 1952. Immediately, Maverick charges, Commissioner of Immigration Argyle R. Mackey in Washington issued "lurid, inflammatory and prejudicial statements that were released to all press associations and around the world," branding Sciortino as a fugitive Italian bandit. Typical headlines: Italy 'Bandit' Now Awaiting Deportation . . . U. S. Airman Held As Sicilian Gang Member.

Maverick assailed the Commissioner's action in an administrative appeal, the only kind available. "Thus," the attorney stated in the appeal brief, "the pool of justice is poisoned from which only poisoned fish can rise. Certainly fair trial was therefore detrimentally influenced . . . This is inherently wrong, is no moral benefit to our country anywhere in the world, and a poor example."

Sciortino, dismayed at the blast of publicity against him, wrote a detailed account of his side of the case for the press. When his account appeared in the San Antonio *Evening News,* Maverick says, Sciortino was placed in "the hole," a high-walled solitary confinement cell.

Sciortino's immigration hearing was held in the county jail—a practice described by Maverick as uncustomary and unusual in American procedure. He was ordered deported, and held without bond. When Maverick sought judicial relief through habeas corpus, the immigration hearing officer was a prosecuting witness against Sciortino!

Maverick appealed to the Board of Immigration Appeals and in his brief spoke of the inherent dangers of such methods as characterized this case:

"The tendency in America today to have one administrative agency decide all, is dangerous to our national welfare, our liberty and to every human being in our country. Unfortunately, although Mr. Mackey is not any Iron Curtain character, but a good man and good American, his precedent of denouncing with vast power, then trying a powerless young man, keeping the man in his own jail, *is not paralleled by any part of the American Government.*

"Did the OPA and lately OPS put men in jail, and keep them there without bond, and try them with 'administrative procedures' by officers of their own who were prosecutors?

"Certainly not.

"Does the Department of Agriculture, in its administrative procedures, keep farmers in jail without bond and try them in jail by its own prosecutors?

"Certainly not.

"If the Immigration Service gets away with this travesty on justice, it is a serious danger to the success of administrative procedures . . . It is clearly to say, and repeat again and again, *the President of the United States has no such power* (and has never tried to use it), neither has the FBI, the Secret Service, Agriculture, Labor (Do you, when settling a strike, keep people in jail with the Labor Department prosecuting inside the jail?), Commerce, or any other Department.

"Sometimes Mr. Edgar Hoover and the FBI are criticized for alleged harshness or great power. *But there are no Hoover jails, no FBI jails.* Mr. Hoover has 'to make a case'; the defendant has the benefit of the courts and bond, and Mr. Hoover must convict before an impartial jury, a fair judge and not by his own men, keeping men in jails and trying them with 'administrative procedure.'

"If judicial procedures are defeated by alleged 'administrative procedures' by the Immigration Service, and the precedent established—then liberties are beginning to be whittled away from businessmen, labor-union men, workers of all kinds, all Americans of any kind. Eventually, if the process continues, it will be decided that the usual courts are outmoded, as they are in the Iron Curtain countries—and then nobody will have a chance—just as Sciortino hasn't had a chance from the start."

Maverick's plea that the "great American democratic

tradition of political asylum should not be reversed" in Sciortino's case was of no avail. (Even if the Board of Immigration Appeals, which exists at the will of the attorney general, had granted the appeal, the attorney general could have overruled the board, for the attorney general's word is final. Since immigration officials act in behalf of the attorney general, the attorney general in effect determines an appeal from his own decision.)

Sciortino, father of a United States citizen child, was deported to Italy early in 1953. And there an Italian court tried him on the charges with which Commissioner Mackey had blasted him in the American press. Sciortino was acquitted on all counts.

It would seem that an attitude of hostility toward aliens is condoned—even, some feel, fostered and encouraged— in the service. For one example, an armed immigration investigator took a Mexican national, unarmed, into custody at a San Joaquin Valley ranch one day in 1952. He forced the Mexican to crawl on his hands and knees and stomach down a hot paved road, in front of the investigator's slowly moving car, until he collapsed. When the incident—characterized by the Mexican consul at Fresno as "sadistic and degrading"—was exposed in the newspapers, the district director offered the investigator's explanation that he had to do this because his handcuffs weren't working.

Despite this—and all that has been related so far— Commissioner of Immigration Mackey, in reply to a criticism of the service several years ago, insisted that the service "endeavors at all times to enforce the law fairly

and humanely." He proudly referred critics to A REMINDER
that is posted in every office of the service:

Our Greatness Is Measured By Our Kindness.

Our Real Calibre Is Measured By the Consideration and
Tolerance We Have for Others.

Chapter

20 In his Executive Order setting up the President's Commission in September of 1952, President Truman asked the group to study and evaluate "the effect of our immigration laws and their administration, including the national origin quota system, on the conduct of the foreign policy of the United States."

The Commission found: "American immigration policies have frustrated and handicapped the aims and programs of American foreign policy throughout the period since 1924. The interference is acute today. The contradictions are sharper now in part because the 1952 law is more restrictive than before. The major factor, however, is the new circumstance of American leadership in the world rivalry between democratic freedom and Communist tyranny."

It was in 1924 that we added Japanese to the Oriental exclusion list. And it was onto the 1924 Immigration Act that the national origin formula with its racist implications was tacked.

This was the Era of Isolation. America for Americans.

Let the rest of the world go by. We had withdrawn, turtle-like, into our continental shell.

We came out again for World War II. And we won, with victory, the mantle of free world leadership, a role we now recognized and accepted. And there was still a job to do. Hitler and his Nazi dream of global conquest lay in ruins. But a new menace showed. Stalin quickly vassalized Eastern Europe—Communism was on the rampage.

We lavished money and technicians and materials to stem this tide and bolster the free nations against further onslaught. It would seem that we thus broadcast our belief in the concept that a human being, wherever he lived, was entitled to certain inalienable rights—to life, liberty and the pursuit of happiness.

Our role was effective—up to a point. It diked the Red flood in Europe. But after providing the funds to implement the Marshall Plan foreign policy that stayed this tide, Congress curiously enough began tearing down American prestige and good will abroad with an immigration policy that affronts foreign nations and individuals alike, and contradicts the concept of the dignity of the human being, wherever he lives.

Monsignor L. G. Ligutti, executive director of the National Catholic Rural Life Conference, told the President's Commission:

"I have had occasion to travel far and wide throughout the world. I have met many friends of the United States. I have also met people who honestly suspect our motives and our sincerity. I have heard the following statements made: 'Hitler tore pages from the United States Congressional Record when he shouted forth his claims of Teutonic racial superiority.' 'Is democracy, which you Americans present as the salvation of the world, based upon the unity and equality of the human race, or do you define it to suit your own conveniences and prejudices at various times and places?'

"The work of UNRRA, Marshall Plan, ECA, MSA, and all assistance given to Italy, Greece, Turkey, and other nations have saved Western Europe from Communism. The majority of the people there are deeply grateful and appreciative. The implications of the McCarran-Walter bill as they were discussed and analyzed at the end of last June [1952] in the continental European press practically erased the great good that has been done. Communist papers headlined the news, 'We told you so.'"

Some historians believe that the Japanese Exclusion Act, by generating a face-saving hate-America excess culminating in the Asia-for-Asiatics doctrine, was an important factor that led to the war in the Pacific. The McCarran Act finally removed the last vestige of Oriental exclusion as an outright policy, but it retained and even enlarged upon the old racist features. And the Chinese Communists have not been reluctant to make propaganda of it.

Philip M. Hauser, professor of sociology at the University of Chicago, who had just returned from a fourteen-month overseas journey, told the President's Commission that the new act was well known to the peoples of the world.

"It does untold damage to the United States in creating attitudes of distrust and hostility," he said. ". . . We have unwittingly placed into the hands of the ruthless, adroit, and unscrupulous propagandists of the U.S.S.R. a major weapon with which to attack us. As a resident of South-eastern Asia for about a year, I had occasion to listen to Radio Moscow and to read the local news reports of the activities of Russian agents and propagandists. In this critical area, the fate of which may well determine the fate of the world, the U.S.S.R. is skillfully and continuously making the most of our ethnic and racist doctrines as promulgated in Public Law 414."

Not only foreign scientists, but businessmen, journalists, writers and artists of distinction have felt the sting of our visa policy under this law. And when any of these persons, esteemed in their own countries, fall victim of our immigration law the repercussions in the foreign press are loud.

People of all faiths and stations deplored the harmful effect of the immigration law on our foreign policy. Among them were W. Averell Harriman, former director of Mutual Security; Edward M. O'Connor, consultant to the Psychological Strategy Board; Anna Lord Straus, past president of the League of Women Voters; Mrs. Z. W. Schroeder, of the General Federation of Women's Clubs; A. B. Kline, president of the American Farm Bureau Federation; the late Philip Murray, president of the CIO; Mrs. Mildred McAfee Horton, of the National Council of Churches of Christ, formerly president of Wellesley College and director of the WAVES; Dr. Paul C. Empie, executive director, National Lutheran Council; Archbishop Richard J. Cushing of Boston, and Lester Gutterman, of the Anti-Defamation League of B'nai B'rith.

The Governments of Canada, the United Kingdom, and the Philippine Republic have protested through diplomatic channels certain features of the act.

Former Secretary of State Dean Acheson, affirming that immigration "is closely linked with our foreign policy and objectives," told the Commission that our immigration policy "causes resentment" among our neighbors in the Caribbean "whom we need as strong partners and who can furnish us with sites for military bases and strategic raw materials." He said "our discriminatory policies" were feeding the propaganda mill of anti-American nationalist papers in Africa, and were engendering "soreness and doubt" in Europe that "inhibit progress toward mutual trust."

Said Professor Carl Friedrich of Harvard: "One of the most unfortunate things that we have done was the provision in the McCarran Act by which aliens were barred from coming to this country because of membership in organizations objectionable for one reason or another to people in this country.

"You probably heard about the reaction in Italy where somebody got up in the Parliament and said he wished to introduce a law that the consulates in the United States be instructed that no one could be granted a visa to Italy from the United States who had belonged to the Ku Klux Klan or any other anti-democratic organization."

Chapter

21 What can be done about the denial of due process to the alien in our midst? And the stranger at our golden door—is he not entitled to *any* rights? And wherever a man is born on the face of the earth, is he not a part of mankind?

In view of America's position in the family of nations, the following thoughts are offered:

Visas

A visa, hard come by, should be tantamount to a welcome to the United States. Therefore, a person arriving with a visa, be he guest or future citizen, should be greeted with a courtesy and hospitality proper to such a host as Uncle Sam.

Let's suppose a suspicion arises after he gets his visa. Then let his removal from ship to detention quarters merely be designated a "landing," as it is not now designated.

That simple process would entitle the person, be he even "wretched refuse" from a foreign shore, to the rights of an alien subject to deportation. An alien in America—

criminal, subversive, or whatever—cannot be expelled without a hearing.

A visitor or an immigrant, with a visa, should be entitled to as much before he is excluded. Can such a courtesy imperil a nation whose basic export commodity is advertised as fair play? Justice Jackson, if you need an authority, says the lack of fair play itself poses a real threat to the nation. Remember, this newcomer is not "at large"; he would *simply be told why he is excluded or held in indefinite confinement, and given a chance to defend himself.*

Consuls

Consular officers should be stripped of their absolute power to deny a visa without a review of any kind.

Duplication

A consular officer of the State Department grants a visa after a careful screening of the immigrant. When the visa-bearer arrives at an American port, an immigration officer of the Justice Department screens him all over again and, as often happens, may deny him entry.

Both officials operate under the *same* law.

This duplication should be eliminated. It is costly enough to the individual American taxpayer, but it is far more costly, in anguish as well as cash outlay, to the individual immigrant.

The President's Commission suggests that the administration of the immigration laws be transferred from these two departments to an independent agency along the lines of the Interstate Commerce Commission and the Federal Power Commission. It therefore offered a proposal to create a single, independent Commission on Immigration and Naturalization, appointed by the President, subject to Senate confirmation. This body would have a top administrator, with the duty of administering all phases of the immigration law, in the United States and overseas.

"The duties are so important, particularly in connection with the visa allocation authority," said the President's Commission, "that the public interest requires a definite pin-pointing of responsibility, as well as the full-time attention which a cabinet officer cannot give. The Commission believes that the creation by Congress of a new and independent immigration agency will assure the development of the fresh approach needed to change our immigration policy from a negative to a positive force."

Hearings

The law should decree, in clear and unmistakable language, that the Immigration Service conduct its hearings in conformity with requirements of the Administrative Procedure Act.

The American Bar Association has spearheaded the fight for fair hearings. Its representative told the President's Commission: "The provisions of the Administrative Procedure Act taken in their entirety represent a careful, well-considered view of the minimal procedural protection needed in a trial involving accusatory elements. This is not less but indeed more true of deportation proceedings than of other proceedings to which the Administrative Procedure Act is applicable. The interest of a person about to be deported and of his relatives and close friends is among the weightiest and most significant that can be imagined."

Appeals

An alien who has been ordered deported and has exhausted the administrative remedies available should have the right of *appeal to the courts*—and not simply the constitutional right of a limited habeas corpus review. In exclusion cases, there should be the right of appeal, if not to the courts, then at least to an impartial board.

The President's Commission advocated the creation of a Board of Immigration and Visa Appeals, established by law, to handle all appeals in exclusion, deportation and visa cases. The present Board of Immigration Appeals, not set up by law, exists at the will of the attorney general, who can reverse decisions of the board. The board proposed by the President's Commission would have final authority, which would be subject only to limited appeal to the Commission on Immigration and Naturalization.

Justice

The statute of limitations should be restored to deportation actions.

Retroactive and *ex post facto* features of the present law should be abolished.

A clearer, and more humane, definition of hardship in deportation cases is called for.

An alien in the United States, technically in violation of the immigration law but otherwise eligible for permanent residence, should not be forced to make an expensive trip to his native land simply to purge that error and pick up a visa entitling him to come right back. He should be able to have his immigration status adjusted here.

A re-entry permit, with a proper regard for semantics, should mean just that—a *re-entry* permit.

What makes an immigrant "likely at any time to become a public charge" should not be left to the mere opinion of a consular or immigration officer. It should be based on findings of fact rather than on an opinion or belief.

Regulatory provisions should be more reasonable. For example, failure to notify the attorney general within ten days of a change of address should be a misdemeanor, but not a deportable offense.

Security

All totalitarians should be barred, not just Communists. The present law does not ban Nazis or Fascists.

The definition of what constitutes affiliation with subversive organizations should be more flexible. For instance, the present law makes no exception for involuntary or nominal, long-forgotten membership in a political party or organization.

Quotas

The National Origin Quota Formula should be abolished. A new system should be devised that will eliminate all the racial aspects of the present law that heap so much criticism on the United States.

To be realistic, the quotas should be based on the 1950 census. They are currently based on the 1920 population figure.

When it set a ceiling of roughly 155,000 quota immigrants a year, Congress conceded that the United States could absorb at least that many, well below the mark set by economists. Then why not let them come? Less than 25 per cent of the annual quotas have been utilized in the twenty years to 1953. The surplus— more than 75 per cent —went to waste!

One student of the problem proposes that the unused original quotas of a given year be reallocated proportionately in the following year to those countries which exhausted their quotas. By easing the population tensions of countries like Italy and Greece, it would strengthen their economy, make them less susceptible to Communist propaganda, and in turn bolster our own foreign policy.

Ample other evidence exists that acceptance of the total annual quota limit will benefit the United States. Economists say we must look forward to a declining native population and consequently we need immigration to man our nation. National gross income will be boosted by moderate immigration, thus bettering the standard of living. And there is an adequate food supply.

The minimum quotas allotted to some countries of only 100 per year—no more than a token gesture at best— could easily be boosted to 1,000 without any adverse effect.

Professors and others who were in the nonquota category prior to the 1952 act should be returned to that status. And close relatives of citizens and aliens admitted for permanent residence—spouses, children (adopted and stepchildren), parents and grandparents—should be nonquota, to avoid the hardship of a wait, often years, to get on a nation's quota list.

Charges against future quotas resulting from admissions under the Displaced Persons program should be eliminated.

When an alien is granted a suspension of a deportation order, a quota number is deducted from the quota of the country of his origin. Such an alien should be nonquota, not only to prevent hardship to him and his family, but to preserve the quota rights of those desiring to immigrate.

All the discriminatory features implicit in the Asia-Pacific triangle and the small special quotas allotted to colonies in this hemisphere should be abolished.

As a substitute for the National Origin Formula, the President's Commission recommended a unified quota system—a single quota of one-sixth of 1 per cent of the total population of the United States, instead of the set fragments of the eighty-five national quotas now in effect. It further suggested that the population base be always the latest available census figure, and include all persons in the United States, without regard to national origin, race, color, or creed. On the basis of the 1950 census, this would raise the quota ceiling to about 250,000 a year.

Citizenship

All distinctions between native-born and naturalized citizens, which now create a class of inferior citizens among the foreign-born, should be abolished. Naturalization should be revocable only for an act found by a court to have constituted fraud in the procurement of citizenship.

The power vested in consular officers to determine the citizenship claim of a person abroad, without judicial review, should be limited to a *prima facie* showing that the person had a legitimate claim to United States nationality. The claimant would then be permitted to come to the United States, where his claim may be determined by the Immigration Service. Any denial, either by the consulate or by an immigration official here, should be subject to judicial review.

The suggested changes that would make our immigration laws more humane—more in keeping with the changing times and fundamental American principles— are almost endless.

There is hope that something may be done about it in the second session of the 83rd Congress. In the final day of its first session, legislation was introduced in both Houses designed to erase the "cruelty and inequity" of the McCarran Act, and to raise the "red-tape curtain" from the immigration machinery. This proposed new law, an omnibus bill that comprehensively revises Public Law 414, would be a codification distinguished for two major objectives—greater justice and greater simplicity. It represents eight months of labor by teams of experts, immigration lawyers, and law professors of Harvard and the University of Pennsylvania. Many of the points made here, as well as many of the recommendations made by the President's Commission, are embodied in this new legislation.

There seems no doubt that Congress would do well to heed the advice of the President's Commission—advice formulated after the Commission had heard all sides of the question. This advice was that the immigration law be completely revised and re-written, from the beginning to the end.

Let us keep out the undesirables, of course. Keep out the criminal, the hopelessly diseased and insane, the real subversive who would destroy our way of life.

Let us enact a law that will never again inspire such a letter as was written by the chiefs of five Indian tribes to Senator Humphrey during the debate on the McCarran-Walter Act:

"Dear Senator Humphrey:

"As America's only non-immigrants, we would like to go on record as being opposed to the major aspects of the McCarran immigration bill . . . We are against this bill because of its basic philosophy . . . which accepts and provides for the continuance of racial discrimination. To this we are unalterably opposed . . .

"As American Indians we are not immediately threatened by laws to stop immigration and to deport men and women born abroad. Sometimes we wish we had established such a law in 1492 . . ."

ABOUT THE AUTHOR

JOHN CAMPBELL BRUCE was born in 1906 in Helvetia, a small Pennsylvania mining town. The son of a mine foreman, he tried loading coal in a mine one summer vacation, but after five days, at about forty cents a day, his back and his mining ambitions gave out.

He spent a year at Allegheny College in Pennsylvania, then continued his formal education at San Jose State College in California. For the past twenty-six years Mr. Bruce has been a California newspaperman, the last eleven years as a reporter on the San Francisco *Chronicle*. During the war Mr. Bruce was with the OWI in China.